EVERYDAY VEGAN

GOOD
HOUSEKEEPING

EVERYDAY VEGAN

85+ PLANT-BASED RECIPES

★ GOOD FOOD GUARANTEED ★

HEARST
books

HEARSTBOOKS

An Imprint of Sterling Publishing Co., Inc.
1166 Avenue of the Americas
New York, NY 10036

ISBN 978-1-61837-256-7

The Good Housekeeping Cookbook Seal guarantees that the recipes in this publication
meet the strict standards of the Good Housekeeping Research Institute.
The Institute has been a source of reliable information and a consumer advocate since 1900,
and established its seal of approval in 1909. Every recipe in this publication
has been triple-tested for ease, reliability, and great taste by the Institute.

Hearst Communications, Inc. has made every effort to ensure that all information
in this publication is accurate. However, due to differing conditions, tools, and individual
skills, Hearst Communications, Inc. cannot be responsible for any injuries, losses,
and/or damages that may result from the use of any information in this publication.

Distributed in Canada by Sterling Publishing
c/o Canadian Manda Group, 664 Annette Street
Toronto, Ontario, M6S 2C8, Canada
Distributed in Australia by NewSouth Books
45 Beach Street, Coogee, NSW 2034, Australia

For information about custom editions, special sales, and premium and corporate purchases,
please contact Sterling Special Sales at 800-805-5489 or specialsales@sterlingpublishing.com.

Manufactured in China

2 4 6 8 10 9 7 5 3 1

goodhousekeeping.com
sterlingpublishing.com

Cover design by Scott Russo
Interior design by Sharon Jacobs and Barbara Balch
Photography credits on page 126

CONTENTS

Sweet Potato Cakes with Kale & Bean Salad (page 52)

Foreword

"I'm a vegan" were words that struck fear into the heart of this young Le Cordon Bleu graduate back in the late 1970s. Fresh from a world of julienning, mother sauces, and soufflés, I had moved into a household with a group of friends and agreed to cook once a week. What I didn't know is that I'd be cooking vegan. After a few of my friends' dinners of wallpaper paste–like millet and barley with steamed vegetables, I decided there had to be vegan life beyond this tamari-soaked fare. And there was.

Growing up in an Italian-American family, I ate lots of truly delicious vegetable-based meals, although many contained dairy. So when it came time to cook without meat, seafood, or dairy, I took inspiration from my roots and prepared a pot of vegetable-rich minestrone that everyone enjoyed—me included.

These days, though I'm an omnivore, I cook a lot of meatless meals. Like you, I find that I'm not hungry for meat every night, and less meat means more room for wholesome grains and veggies. The truth is that you can prepare the dishes your family regularly enjoys—pastas and stir-fries, soups and stews, sandwiches and bowls—vegan style. You just have to become familiar with the appropriate substitutions and keep basic nutritional guidelines in mind (page 10).

This collection of simple and satisfying recipes is your road map to delicious vegan meals and snacks. This book opens with energizing breakfasts—from smoothies to granola and, yes, even muffins, pancakes, and waffles for Sunday brunch. Our super salads are paired with suggestions for adding extra grains and protein, and our sandwiches—from Falafel Wraps to Tempeh Reubens with a homemade Thousand Island Dressing—will make lunchtime as yummy as it is healthy. We offer an assortment of nourishing noodle dishes, tofu stir-fries, bean- and veggie-based soups, and tacos you'll be happy to present to family and friends. Because locating a vegan snack when you need it can prove to be a challenge, our sweet and savory treats are easy-to-make nibbles to have on hand when you need a boost of energy.

So whether you're embracing a true vegan lifestyle, cooking for someone who is vegan, or simply looking for more vegetable- and grain-based recipes, *Good Housekeeping Everyday Vegan* provides delicious, easy-to-make recipes that will be a welcome addition to your repertoire.

SUSAN WESTMORELAND
Food Director, *Good Housekeeping*

Introduction

Why Should You Become Vegan?

A vegan diet eliminates all animal products (meat, poultry, and fish) and products derived from animals (butter, milk, yogurt, eggs and cheese). The bonus? This diet naturally encourages you and your family to fill up on good-for-you foods grown from the earth. Study after study has shown that a diet rich in whole grains, legumes, vegetables, and fruit results in numerous health benefits. Some benefits include:

• **A reduced risk of heart disease and a positive effect on those who already have heart disease.** Saturated fat and cholesterol are two dietary culprits that raise the risk for heart disease. Both are derived almost exclusively from animal products.

• **A reduced risk of some cancers.** That's one reason the American Cancer Society recommends eating five or more servings of vegetables and fruits each day. This is easier than you might think: One serving equals 1 cup leafy vegetables, ½ cup cooked or raw vegetables, or ½ cup or one medium piece of fruit.

• **Weight loss and long-term weight management.** Why? Switching to a plant-based diet may dramatically reduce fat and calorie intake. Although there are obese vegans (and slim meat-eaters), the Academy of Nutrition and Dietetics reports lower levels of obesity, reduced risk of heart disease, and lower blood pressure for vegetarians and vegans alike.

Including more whole grains, legumes, vegetables, and fruits also means increasing your intake of fiber, vitamins and minerals, antioxidants, and phytochemicals. That's good news for your diet—and your health!

Benefits for Your Wallet

Adding more produce and grains to your diet and reducing animal products is not only good for your health; it's undeniably good for your pocketbook, too. This is especially true if you primarily prepare your meals with whole foods—grains, beans, and legumes, bought in bulk, and fresh vegetables and fruits rather than processed, canned, frozen, or otherwise packaged ingredients. But even if you rely on packaged tofu and canned beans for your protein, you'll save money.

• **Tofu versus Chicken Breast:** If you're looking for an economical source of protein, tofu costs 40 percent less than chicken breasts. You'll find that it's a versatile choice that can be substituted in a wide variety of your favorite stir-fries, pastas, sandwiches, and casseroles, too.

• **Beans versus Ground Beef:** Beans can't be beat when it comes to a low-cost source of good nutrition. They are packed with protein and insoluble and soluble fiber, and, unlike beef, they contain zero saturated fat and cholesterol. The good news for your wallet: You can purchase almost three cans of beans for the cost of one pound of ground beef.

But don't overlook the money-saving benefits of buying in bulk. Purchase dried beans and legumes instead of canned for one-third of the cost. For convenience, cook them ahead of time using package instructions, then divide into 1½ cup portions (the equivalent of a 15.5-ounce can of beans), pack in airtight containers, and freeze for up to 6 months.

Coconut-Cauliflower Curry Bowls, page 93

Benefits for the Planet

Many people are reducing their consumption of animal products for reasons that extend far beyond their waistlines. They know that following a vegan diet not only delivers individual health benefits, but it also helps ensure a healthier planet for future generations. Consider the following facts:

• **Feeding more people:** It takes more land, water, and energy to produce meat than to grow vegetables and grains. In fact, a study by the Alan Shawn Feinstein World Hunger Program at Brown University found that if we all received 25 percent of our calories from animal products, the global food supply would feed 3.16 billion people, whereas if we all followed a vegetarian diet, we could produce enough food to feed almost twice as many people—6.26 billion! World hunger is a complicated problem, and eating vegan here in the United States won't necessarily alleviate it in the short term, but many people have decided that they want to consume more grains themselves instead of feeding those grains to cows to produce beef.

• **For the love of animals:** You've heard it in the news: Once upon a time, farm animals were raised on small family farms, where they grazed on pastureland or ate locally grown feed and were slaughtered by the same farmer who took care of them. But the competition to produce inexpensive meat, eggs, and dairy products has replaced these small farms with factory farms—large feedlots where animals are raised in confined quarters and treated with antibiotics to avoid the spread of diseases, then shipped off to giant slaughterhouses. Concerned about the treatment of these farm animals and the quality of the products raised on these farms, many people have decided to avoid meat and dairy produced on factory farms by buying locally produced, often organic, alternatives, or by eliminating meat and dairy from their diets altogether.

So when you pass up a beef burger in favor of a veggie burger, you're not only keeping your cholesterol levels down; in a small way, you're helping to ensure the health and well-being of your world.

JACLYN R. LONDON, M.S., R.D.
Nutrition Director, GH Institute

Nutritional Guidelines for Vegans

If you are eliminating meat and dairy from your diet,
there are several nutrients you need to pay particular attention to:

PROTEIN

Necessary for healthy cell function in the human body, including the production of antibodies and hemoglobin, protein is a vegan's first concern. But there is no need; there are plenty of plant-based sources for protein. Pulses (including peas, lentils, garbanzo beans, black beans, and pinto beans), nuts and nut butters, and soy products such as tofu, tempeh, and soy milk are all great sources.

IRON

The iron found in meat and fish is readily absorbed by the body. When on a vegan diet, though, you must rely on iron in plant-based sources. The body has a harder time absorbing the nutrients from these sources. However, when plant-based, iron-rich foods are consumed in tandem with foods containing vitamin C, then the absorption rate increases significantly. Many vegetables contain both, including Brussels sprouts, green peas, shiitake mushrooms, parsley, and leafy greens like kale, spinach, and Swiss chard. Iron enables red blood cells to carry oxygen throughout the body.

CALCIUM

This mineral is used for building bones and teeth; it is also important for maintaining bone strength. Sources of calcium include soybeans and soy-based products like tofu and calcium-enriched soy milk. Some dark leafy greens, like bok choy and collard, turnip, and mustard greens, also contain calcium, but these greens should not be relied on as a primary source.

ZINC

The body does not need much zinc, but it is vital for good health. It is necessary for many biochemical reactions and also helps the immune system function properly. Sources of zinc include many types of beans (chickpeas, white beans, and kidney beans, to name a few) and pumpkin and sesame seeds.

VITAMIN B_{12}

This vitamin is vital to red blood cell production as well as the development of nerve cells. In a vegan diet, it can be found in nutritional yeast, as well as B_{12}-fortified products such as cereal, soymilk, and some veggie burgers.

Granola-Yogurt Parfait
(page 19)

1 Breakfast

Rise and shine! This chapter contains a delicious selection of vegan breakfast and brunch options that are well worth waking up for. If you're looking for quick and easy, search no further. For a perfect on-the-go breakfast, try our smoothies, which feature a bonanza of fruit, plus your choice of nondairy milk or yogurt. Reduced-Fat Granola and Whole-Grain Carrot Cake Muffins will also get you out the door in a jiffy—with a healthy dose of dietary fiber to keep you feeling satisfied until lunchtime. On weekends, when a more leisurely pace is possible, treat family and friends to our South-of-the-Border Veggie Hash or Tofu Scramble with Chopped Tomatoes & Chives. And, yes, you can eat your fill of our Whole-Grain Pancakes, too. Don't forget to bring out the maple syrup (or other delicious vegan toppings) and grab a fork!

Tropical
SMOOTHIE BOWL

Top this fruity smoothie with chopped almonds, shredded coconut, and fresh kiwi, mango, and blueberries.

ACTIVE TIME: 5 MINUTES   **TOTAL TIME:** 5 MINUTES   **MAKES:** 2 SERVINGS

1   banana, sliced and frozen
1   cup frozen mango chunks
1   cup frozen pineapple chunks
1   cup almond milk

In a blender, pulse banana, mango, and pineapple with almond milk until the mixture is smooth but still thick, stopping and stirring occasionally. Add more liquid if needed. Pour into 2 bowls. Top as desired.

EACH SERVING: ABOUT 180 CALORIES, 3G PROTEIN, 43G CARBOHYDRATE, 2G TOTAL FAT (0G SATURATED), 5G FIBER, 90MG SODIUM

Berry-Coconut
SMOOTHIE BOWL

The ingredients in this super smoothie pack plenty of natural sweetness.

ACTIVE TIME: 5 MINUTES   **TOTAL TIME:** 5 MINUTES   **MAKES:** 2 SERVINGS

1   banana, sliced and frozen
2   cups frozen mixed berries
1   cup coconut water

Blend banana and mixed berries with coconut water. Pour into 2 bowls. Top as desired.

EACH SERVING: ABOUT 160 CALORIES, 2G PROTEIN, 39G CARBOHYDRATE, 1G TOTAL FAT (0G SATURATED), 7G FIBER, 3MG SODIUM

Orange Sunrise
SMOOTHIE

Make this once and you'll want it to start all your mornings.

ACTIVE TIME: 5 MINUTES   TOTAL TIME: 5 MINUTES   MAKES: 1¾ CUPS OR 1 SERVING

1   cup vanilla soy milk

¼   cup frozen orange juice concentrate

2   tablespoons orange marmalade

2   ice cubes

In a blender, combine soy milk, orange juice concentrate, marmalade, and ice; blend until the mixture is smooth and frothy. Pour into a tall glass.

EACH SERVING: ABOUT 360 CALORIES, 8G PROTEIN, 73G CARBOHYDRATE, 5G TOTAL FAT (0G SATURATED), 2G FIBER, 144MG SODIUM

Pomegranate–Berry
SMOOTHIE

A delicious and healthful breakfast. Berries and pomegranates are loaded with heart-healthy antioxidants.

ACTIVE TIME: 5 MINUTES   TOTAL TIME: 5 MINUTES   MAKES: 2 CUPS OR 1 SERVING

½   cup pomegranate juice, chilled

½   cup nondairy vanilla yogurt

1   cup frozen mixed berries

In a blender, combine juice, yogurt, and berries; blend until the mixture is smooth. Pour into a tall glass.

EACH SERVING: ABOUT 230 CALORIES, 5G PROTEIN, 50G CARBOHYDRATE, 3G TOTAL FAT (0G SATURATED), 5G FIBER, 25MG SODIUM

Banana–Peanut Butter
SMOOTHIE

For a thicker, colder smoothie, cut peeled banana into chunks and freeze for up to one week in a zip-seal plastic bag.

ACTIVE TIME: 5 MINUTES · **TOTAL TIME:** 5 MINUTES · **MAKES:** 1½ CUPS OR 1 SERVING

1 small ripe banana, cut in half

½ cup soy milk

1 teaspoon creamy peanut butter

3 ice cubes

In a blender, combine banana, soy milk, peanut butter, and ice cubes; blend until the mixture is smooth and frothy. Pour into a tall glass.

EACH SERVING: ABOUT 165 CALORIES, 6G PROTEIN, 28G CARBOHYDRATE, 4G TOTAL FAT (2G SATURATED), 2G FIBER, 85MG SODIUM

Mighty Veggie
SMOOTHIE

Don't let the name throw you! This fabulous blend of supersweet beets, carrots, orange juice, and frozen bananas is a delicious way to power up—and get your veggies.

ACTIVE TIME: 5 MINUTES · **TOTAL TIME:** 5 MINUTES · **MAKES:** 2 SERVINGS

4 small refrigerated cooked beets, sliced

¾ cup shredded carrots

1 cup orange juice

2 frozen ripe bananas, cut up

1 tablespoon ground flaxseeds

In a blender, combine beets, carrots, orange juice, bananas, and flaxseeds; blend until mixture is smooth and frothy. Pour into 2 glasses.

EACH SERVING: ABOUT 232 CALORIES, 5G PROTEIN, 53G CARBOHYDRATE, 2G TOTAL FAT (0G SATURATED), 7G FIBER, 94MG SODIUM

REDUCED-FAT
Granola

We baked a vegan granola with just a fraction of the fat
by using apple juice instead of oil and butter.

ACTIVE TIME: 10 MINUTES   TOTAL TIME: 35 MINUTES   MAKES: 6 CUPS OR 12 SERVINGS

4   cups old-fashioned oats, uncooked

½   cup maple syrup

½   cup apple juice

1½   teaspoons vanilla extract

¾   teaspoon ground cinnamon

½   cup natural almonds

½   cup quinoa, thoroughly rinsed

¼   cup toasted wheat germ

2   tablespoons sesame seeds

½   cup dried apricots,
     cut into ¼-inch pieces

½   cup dark seedless raisins

1 Preheat your oven to 350°F. Place the oats in two 15½ x 10½-inch jelly-roll pans. Bake until lightly toasted, about 15 minutes, stirring twice.

2 In a large bowl, with a wire whisk, mix the maple syrup, apple juice, vanilla, and cinnamon until blended. Add the toasted oats, almonds, quinoa, wheat germ, and sesame seeds; stir well to coat.

3 Spread the oat mixture evenly in the same jelly-roll pans; bake until golden brown, 20 to 25 minutes, stirring frequently. Cool in the pans on a wire rack.

4 Transfer the granola to a large bowl; stir in the apricots and raisins. Store at room temperature in a tightly covered container for up to 1 month.

EACH SERVING: ABOUT 350 CALORIES, 12G PROTEIN, 64G CARBOHYDRATE, 8G TOTAL FAT (2G SATURATED), 8G FIBER, 10MG SODIUM

Granola-Yogurt
PARFAIT

A healthy breakfast doesn't get any easier
(or more delicious) than this. For photo, see page 12.

ACTIVE TIME: 5 MINUTES   **TOTAL TIME:** 5 MINUTES   **MAKES:** 1 SERVING

½   cup fresh or frozen (partially thawed)
    strawberries

¾   cup nondairy vanilla yogurt

2   tablespoons Reduced-Fat Granola
    (opposite)

Into a parfait glass or wineglass, spoon some of
the strawberries, nondairy yogurt, and granola.
Repeat layering until all ingredients are used.

EACH SERVING: ABOUT 295 CALORIES, 8G PROTEIN,
70G CARBOHYDRATE, 21G TOTAL FAT (4G SATURATED),
18G FIBER, 47MG SODIUM

WHOLE-GRAIN **Pancakes**

These pancakes allow you to go egg-free and give you a double dose of whole-grain goodness. Polish off with a delicious pancake topper, below.

ACTIVE TIME: 15 MINUTES **TOTAL TIME:** 30 MINUTES **MAKES:** 4 SERVINGS

1½ cups plain soy milk

⅔ cup quick-cooking oats

½ cup all-purpose flour

½ cup whole wheat flour

2 teaspoons baking powder

¼ teaspoon salt

canola oil

1 In a medium bowl, combine the soy milk and oats. Let stand for 10 minutes.

2 Meanwhile, in a large bowl, combine the all-purpose and whole wheat flours, baking powder, and salt. Stir 3 tablespoons oil into the oat mixture and add to dry ingredients. Stir just until the flour mixture is moistened (batter will be lumpy).

3 Spray a nonstick 12-inch skillet with nonstick cooking spray; heat over medium heat until hot. Making 4 pancakes at a time, pour the batter by scant ¼ cups into a skillet, spreading the batter into 3½-inch circles. Cook until the tops are bubbly and the edges look dry, 2 to 3 minutes. With a wide spatula, turn the pancakes and cook until he undersides are golden brown. Transfer the pancakes to a platter. Cover to keep warm.

4 Repeat with remaining batter, using more cooking spray as needed.

EACH SERVING: ABOUT 300 CALORIES, 8G PROTEIN, 37G CARBOHYDRATE, 14G TOTAL FAT (1G SATURATED), 4G FIBER, 466MG SODIUM

Delicious Pancake Toppers

Maple syrup will always be a classic, but to keep things interesting, try these yummy nondairy toppings.

Fresh seasonal fruit, like raspberries and chopped nectarines, drizzled with **nondairy vanilla yogurt**

Dollops of homemade Almond Ricotta (page 120), plus fresh orange wedges

Toasted nuts (walnuts, pecans, or whatever you have on hand), **sweetened coconut flakes**, and **maple syrup**. Or, for a decadent treat, swap **melted dark chocolate** for the maple syrup (make sure to look for unsweetened cocoa or chocolate—they're always vegan).

Tofu Scramble
WITH CHOPPED TOMATOES & CHIVES

Here's a tasty tofu scramble flecked with tomato and chives
and seasoned with garlic, turmeric, and a dash of lemon juice for zip.

ACTIVE TIME: 15 MINUTES   **TOTAL TIME:** 15 MINUTES   **MAKES:** 4 SERVINGS

1   (14-ounce) package firm tofu

extra-virgin olive oil

1   large garlic clove, finely chopped

¼   cup snipped fresh chives

pinch cayenne pepper

½   teaspoon turmeric

1   large tomato, seeded and chopped

salt

1   tablespoon lemon juice

1 Rinse the tofu and press with a clean towel to absorb excess water. Place in a bowl and mash into small pieces with a fork.

2 In a nonstick 12-inch skillet, heat 3 tablespoons oil over medium heat until hot. Stir in the garlic, chives, cayenne, and turmeric; cook for 2 minutes, stirring.

3 Add the mashed tofu, tomato, and ½ teaspoon salt; raise the heat and simmer for 5 minutes. Remove from heat and stir in lemon juice.

EACH SERVING: ABOUT 190 CALORIES, 9G PROTEIN, 5G CARBOHYDRATE, 15G TOTAL FAT (2G SATURATED), 2G FIBER, 297MG SODIUM

SOUTH-OF-THE-BORDER
Veggie Hash

This savory combination of classic hash ingredients gets a new flavor twist from kidney beans, cilantro, and a squeeze of lime juice. Serve with fruit salad or a smoothie for a brunch that's as easy as it is satisfying.

ACTIVE TIME: 20 MINUTES   **TOTAL TIME:** 50 MINUTES   **MAKES:** 4 SERVINGS

3 large Yukon Gold potatoes (1½ pounds), cut into ¾-inch pieces

olive oil

1 large onion (12 ounces), cut into ¼-inch pieces

1 medium red pepper (4 to 6 ounces), cut into ¼-inch-wide strips

3 garlic cloves, crushed with press

2 teaspoons ground cumin

salt

1 (15- to 19-ounce) can red kidney or black beans, drained and rinsed

2 tablespoons chopped fresh cilantro

nondairy plain yogurt, lime wedges, salsa, and warmed corn tortillas (optional)

1 In a 3-quart saucepan, place the potatoes into enough water to cover; heat to boiling over high heat. Reduce the heat to low; cover and simmer until the potatoes are almost tender, about 5 minutes; drain well.

2 Meanwhile, in a nonstick 12-inch skillet, heat 2 tablespoons oil over medium heat until hot. Add the onion, red pepper, garlic, cumin, and ¾ teaspoon salt; cook for 10 minutes, stirring occasionally. Add the drained potatoes and cook, turning them occasionally, until the vegetables are lightly browned, about 5 minutes longer. Stir in the beans and cook until heated through, 2 minutes longer. Sprinkle with cilantro.

3 Serve the vegetable hash with yogurt, lime wedges, salsa, and tortillas, if you like.

EACH SERVING: ABOUT 360 CALORIES, 12G PROTEIN, 63G CARBOHYDRATE, 8G TOTAL FAT (1G SATURATED), 13G FIBER, 625MG SODIUM

WHOLE-GRAIN
Carrot Cake Muffins

These muffins are as scrumptious as carrot cake but contain good-for-you grains, so you can indulge without guilt.

ACTIVE TIME: 20 MINUTES   **TOTAL TIME:** 45 MINUTES   **MAKES:** 12 MUFFINS

nonstick cooking spray

1   cup quick-cooking oats

1   cup all-purpose flour

½   cup whole wheat flour

½   cup packed brown sugar

2   teaspoons baking powder

½   teaspoon baking soda

½   teaspoon salt

1   teaspoon pumpkin pie spice

1¼ cups plain unsweetened soy milk

¼   cup unsweetened applesauce

canola oil

1   teaspoon vanilla extract

2   cups shredded carrots

½   cup raisins

1   teaspoon granulated sugar

1 Preheat your oven to 400°F. Grease a muffin tin with nonstick cooking spray.

2 Place the oats in a blender and blend until finely ground.

3 In a large bowl, combine the ground oats, all-purpose and whole wheat flours, brown sugar, baking powder, baking soda, salt, and pumpkin pie spice. In a small bowl, with a fork, blend the soy milk, applesauce, 3 tablespoons oil, and vanilla. Stir into the flour mixture until the flour is moistened. Fold in the carrots and raisins.

4 Spoon the batter into the muffin-pan cups (cups will be very full). Sprinkle with granulated sugar. Bake for 23 to 27 minutes or until a toothpick inserted into the center of a muffin comes out clean. Remove to a wire rack; serve warm, or cool to serve later.

EACH SERVING: ABOUT 190 CALORIES, 4G PROTEIN, 35G CARBOHYDRATE, 5G TOTAL FAT (0G SATURATED) 3G FIBER, 270MG SODIUM

Blueberry MUFFINS

When retooling a recipe to be egg-free, oil and/or fruit purees are often used to provide the moistness eggs typically supply. In this recipe, applesauce plays that role.

ACTIVE TIME: 20 MINUTES   TOTAL TIME: 45 MINUTES   MAKES: 12 MUFFINS

1   cup quick-cooking oats

1   cup all-purpose flour

½   cup whole wheat flour

½   cup packed brown sugar

2   teaspoons baking powder

½   teaspoon baking soda

½   teaspoon salt

1¼   cups plain unsweetened soy milk

1¼   cups unsweetened applesauce

canola oil

1   teaspoon vanilla extract

2   cups blueberries

1   teaspoon granulated sugar

1 Preheat your oven to 400°F. Line a 12-cup muffin pan with paper liners.

2 Place the oats in a blender and blend until finely ground.

3 In a large bowl, combine the ground oats, all-purpose and whole wheat flours, brown sugar, baking powder, baking soda, and salt. In a small bowl, with fork, blend soy milk, applesauce, 3 tablespoons oil, and vanilla; stir into the flour mixture until the flour is moistened. Fold in the blueberries.

4 Spoon the batter into the muffin-pan cups (cups will be very full). Sprinkle with the granulated sugar. Bake until a toothpick inserted into the center of a muffin comes out clean, 23 to 25 minutes. Remove to a wire rack; serve warm, or cool to serve later.

EACH SERVING: ABOUT 80 CALORIES, 4G PROTEIN, 31G CARBOHYDRATE, 5G TOTAL FAT (0G SATURATED), 2G FIBER, 254MG SODIUM

TIP

If it's not blueberry season, feel free to substitute frozen blueberries. Just add 3 to 5 minutes to your baking time, as the frozen berries will lower the temperature of your batter from the get-go. Don't thaw the berries before adding them to the batter, or you'll end up with a big purple mess.

Falafel Wraps
(page 36)

2 | Sandwiches

In this chapter, we've provided lots of tempting sandwich ideas, including some fun vegan riffs on classics, like Tempeh Reubens with homemade Thousand Island Dressing and Eggless Egg Salad Sandwiches made using tofu and turmeric. Plus we've included three meat-free burgers filled with delicious vegetables and hearty grains. You'll see that satisfyingly "meaty" burgers can be made from quinoa and mushrooms or portobello mushroom caps. These recipes also offer lots of opportunities to incorporate whole-grain goodness into your lunch hour. Serve a Healthy Club Sandwich on multigrain toast, or choose a whole wheat pita when you make a Falafel Wrap. If a sandwich just isn't a sandwich without mayonnaise, try our yummy tofu-based recipes for Herb Mayonnaise and Aioli.

PORTOBELLO **Burgers**

We marinate these "burgers" in a broth mixture
accented with thyme before grilling.

ACTIVE TIME: 10 MINUTES   **TOTAL TIME:** 30 MINUTES, PLUS STANDING   **MAKES:** 4 SERVINGS

¼   cup vegetable broth

olive oil

2   teaspoons balsamic vinegar

1   teaspoon fresh thyme leaves

salt

ground black pepper

4   medium (about 4-inch) portobello
    mushrooms caps

1   lemon

⅓   cup Vegan Mayonnaise (page 29)

1   small green onion, minced

8   slices sourdough toast

1   bunch arugula, trimmed

1 In a glass baking dish just large enough to
hold the mushrooms in a single layer, mix the
broth, 2 tablespoons oil, vinegar, thyme, and
¼ teaspoon each of salt and pepper. Add the
mushrooms, turning to coat. Let stand for
30 minutes, turning occasionally.

2 Meanwhile, from the lemon, grate ½ teaspoon
peel and squeeze ½ teaspoon juice. In a small
bowl, stir the lemon peel, lemon juice, Vegan
Mayonnaise, green onion, and 1 teaspoon each
of salt and pepper.

3 Prepare an outdoor grill or heat a ridged
grill pan over medium heat until hot. Add the
mushrooms and grill, turning occasionally and
brushing with the remaining marinade, until the
mushrooms are browned and cooked through,
8 to 10 minutes per side.

4 Spread four slices of toast with the mayonnaise
mixture; top with arugula and the warm
mushrooms. Cover with remaining toast.

EACH SERVING: ABOUT 320 CALORIES, 8G PROTEIN,
29G CARBOHYDRATE, 20G TOTAL FAT (4G SATURATED),
3G FIBER, 518MG SODIUM

SOUTHWESTERN
Black Bean Burgers

These zesty burgers will be appreciated by everyone at the barbecue.

ACTIVE TIME: 15 MINUTES   TOTAL TIME: 20 MINUTES   MAKES: 4 SERVINGS

1   (15- to 19-ounce) can black beans, drained and rinsed

2   tablespoons Vegan Mayonnaise

¼   cup loosely packed fresh cilantro leaves, chopped

1   tablespoon plain dried bread crumbs

½   teaspoon ground cumin

½   teaspoon hot pepper sauce

nonstick cooking spray

1   cup loosely packed sliced lettuce

4   (4-inch) mini whole wheat pita breads, warmed

½   cup mild salsa

1   Prepare an outdoor grill for direct grilling over medium heat.

2   In a large bowl, with a potato masher or fork, mash the black beans with the Vegan Mayonnaise until almost smooth (some lumps of beans should remain). Stir in the cilantro, bread crumbs, cumin, and hot pepper sauce until combined. With lightly floured hands, shape the bean mixture into four 3-inch round patties. Spray both sides of each patty lightly with cooking spray.

3   Place the burgers on a hot grill rack over medium heat. Grill the burgers until lightly browned, about 6 minutes, turning once.

4   Arrange the lettuce on pitas; top with the burgers and salsa.

EACH SERVING: ABOUT 265 CALORIES, 11G PROTEIN, 42G CARBOHYDRATE, 6G TOTAL FAT (1G SATURATED), 11G FIBER, 750MG SODIUM

Vegan Mayonnaise

Combine **½ cup silken tofu, ½ teaspoon Dijon mustard, 2 teaspoons cider vinegar,** and **¼ teaspoon salt** in a blender; blend until completely smooth. Through the hole in the top of the blender, slowly add **1 tablespoon plus 2 teaspoons canola oil**, blending until completely combined. Makes ¾ cup.

Aioli

Add **1 garlic clove**, minced, when blending.

Herb Mayonnaise

Add **1 tablespoon chopped fresh herbs** when blending.

EACH TABLESPOON: ABOUT 25 CALORIES, 1G PROTEIN, 0G CARBOHYDRATE, 2G TOTAL FAT (0G SATURATED), 0G FIBER, 55MG SODIUM

Mushroom Quinoa Burgers
WITH ROSEMARY MAYO

These veggie burgers are hearty enough for carnivores.

ACTIVE TIME: 15 MINUTES   **TOTAL TIME:** 45 MINUTES, PLUS STANDING   **MAKES:** 5 SERVINGS

4 medium portobello mushroom caps (about 1 pound), gills removed, chopped

½ cup walnuts

1 garlic clove

canola oil

salt

ground black pepper

¼ cup red onion, chopped

3 green onions, chopped

2 teaspoons rice wine vinegar

1 cup cooked quinoa

½ cup cornstarch

Rosemary Mayo, whole-grain burger buns, sprouts, lettuce, and sliced tomatoes, for serving

1 Preheat your oven to 375°F. In a 3-quart shallow baking dish, toss the mushrooms with walnuts, garlic, 1 tablespoon oil, ¾ teaspoon salt, and ¼ teaspoon pepper, and spread in even layer. Bake for 20 minutes or until the mushrooms are tender. Set aside to cool. Turn the oven off.

2 In a food processor, pulse the mushroom mixture, red onion, green onions, and vinegar until mostly smooth, scraping the side of the bowl if necessary. Transfer the mixture to a large bowl and stir in quinoa and cornstarch until well-blended. Cover the bowl with plastic wrap and refrigerate for 2 hours.

3 Preheat your oven to 375°F. Line the baking sheet with foil. Form the mixture into 5 patties (about ½ inch thick and 3 inches wide). In a 12-inch nonstick skillet, heat 1 tablespoon oil on medium. In 2 batches, cook the patties for 5 minutes or until well-browned, turning over once. Transfer the seared patties to a prepared baking sheet. Bake for 10 minutes or until hot in centers.

4 Serve the burgers on buns with Rosemary Mayo, garnished with sprouts, lettuce, and tomato.

EACH SERVING: 495 CALORIES, 9G PROTEIN, 49G CARBOHYDRATE, 31G TOTAL FAT (4G SATURATED), 7G FIBER, 700MG SODIUM

Rosemary Mayo

Combine **½ cup Vegan Mayonnaise, 1 teaspoon finely chopped fresh rosemary, 1 teaspoon lemon juice**, and **a pinch of salt**. Keeps for up to 5 days, refrigerated.

EACH SERVING: 495 CALORIES, 9G PROTEIN, 49G CARBOHYDRATE, 31G TOTAL FAT (4G SATURATED), 7G FIBER, 700MG SODIUM

GRILLED CORN & JACK
Quesadillas

These quesadillas make a fun and simple summertime meal.
To save time, grate the cheese for the quesadillas
while the corn is grilling.

ACTIVE TIME: 15 MINUTES   TOTAL TIME: 20 MINUTES, PLUS STANDING   MAKES: 4 SERVINGS

3   large ears corn, husks and silk removed

4   (8- to 10-inch) low-fat flour tortillas

1   cup (4 ounces) soy Monterey Jack cheese,
     shredded

½   cup mild or medium-hot salsa

2   green onions, thinly sliced

1 Prepare an outdoor grill for covered direct
grilling over medium-high heat.
2 Place the corn on the hot grill rack. Cover the
grill and cook the corn, turning frequently, until
brown in spots, 10 to 15 minutes.

3 Transfer the corn to a plate; set aside until it's
cool enough to handle. When cool, cut the kernels
from the cobs with a sharp knife.
4 Place the tortillas on a work surface. Evenly
divide the soy Monterey Jack, salsa, green onions,
and corn on half of each tortilla. Fold the tortilla
over the filling to make 4 quesadillas.
5 Place the quesadillas on the hot grill rack.
Grill the quesadillas, turning once, until browned
on both sides, 1 to 2 minutes. Transfer to a
cutting board; cut each quesadilla into 3 pieces.

EACH SERVING: ABOUT 305 CALORIES, 9G PROTEIN,
50G CARBOHYDRATE, 10G TOTAL FAT (1G SATURATED),
7G FIBER, 689MG SODIUM

ZUCCHINI & BLACK BEAN
Burritos

Here's a quick, dairy-free version of restaurant-style burritos.

vegetable oil

4   medium zucchini (5 ounces each), each cut lengthwise in half, then sliced crosswise

salt

¼   teaspoon ground cinnamon

1   (15-ounce) can Spanish-style red kidney beans

1   (15- to 19-ounce) can black beans, drained and rinsed

4   flour tortillas, 10 inches each

1   cup shredded nondairy Monterey Jack cheese (optional)

½   cup loosely packed fresh cilantro leaves

1   (16-ounce) jar chunky-style salsa, for serving

1 In a 12-inch skillet, heat 2 teaspoons oil over medium-high heat. Add the zucchini, ¼ teaspoon salt, and cinnamon; cook until the zucchini is tender-crisp, about 5 minutes.

2 Meanwhile, in a 2-quart saucepan, heat the kidney beans with their sauce and the black beans over medium heat just to simmering; keep warm.

3 Microwave the tortillas on a plate between paper towels on High for 1 to 2 minutes or until heated through. Allow each person to assemble hiss or her burrito as desired, using a warm flour tortilla; zucchini; bean mixture; cheese, if using; and cilantro leaves. Pass the salsa around to serve with the burritos.

EACH SERVING: ABOUT 480 CALORIES, 19G PROTEIN, 80G CARBOHYDRATE, 10G TOTAL FAT (2G SATURATED), 20G FIBER, 953MG SODIUM

TEMPEH **Reubens**

Seasoned crispy tempeh and luscious Vegan Mayonnaise-based dressing stand in for the corned beef and famous sauce of the original. The end result: complete satisfaction!

ACTIVE TIME: 10 MINUTES   **TOTAL TIME:** 35 MINUTES   **MAKES:** 4 SERVINGS

1   (8-ounce) package tempeh, cut crosswise to make 4 squares

2   garlic cloves

2   cups vegetable broth

1   bay leaf

1   teaspoon ground coriander

1   teaspoon paprika

½   teaspoon ground ginger

ground black pepper

1   ripe avocado, peeled and chopped

canola oil

1   cup sauerkraut, drained well

8   slices rye bread

¼   cup Thousand Island Dressing

1 In a medium saucepan, heat the tempeh, garlic, broth, and bay leaf to boiling over high heat. Reduce the heat to low; cover and simmer for 25 minutes, turning once. Remove the tempeh from the liquid and cool. Discard the liquid, garlic, and bay leaf. Cut each square of tempeh horizontally in half and toss in a bowl with the coriander, paprika, ginger, and 1 teaspoon pepper.

2 In a small bowl, mash the avocado.

3 In a nonstick 12-inch skillet, heat 3 tablespoons oil over medium-high heat until hot. Add the tempeh and cook until browned and crisped, about 7 minutes, turning once.

4 Meanwhile, toast the bread. Spread the mashed avocado onto 4 slices of toasted bread. Top each avocado-covered slice with 2 pieces tempeh and 3 tablespoons sauerkraut. Spread 1 tablespoon dressing onto the remaining 4 slices and place on top of the tempeh slices. Cut in half and serve.

EACH SERVING: ABOUT 465 CALORIES, 19G PROTEIN, 47G CARBOHYDRATE, 24G TOTAL FAT (3G SATURATED), 12G FIBER, 773MG SODIUM

Thousand Island Dressing

In a small bowl, combine **½ cup Vegan Mayonnaise** (page 29), **3 tablespoons ketchup**, **3 teaspoons white wine vinegar**, **2 teaspoons agave syrup**, **¼ teaspoon onion powder**, **4 teaspoons sweet pickle relish**, and **salt** and **ground black pepper** to taste. Whisk together until well blended. Refrigerate for 20 minutes before using.

EACH SERVING: ABOUT 40 CALORIES, 1G PROTEIN, 3G CARBOHYDRATE, 3G TOTAL FAT (0G SATURATED), 0G FIBER, 145MG SODIUM

EGGLESS
Egg Salad Sandwiches

Tofu plays a key role in this dish, absorbing
the seasonings and providing egg-like creaminess.
Turmeric contributes the "egg yolk" yellow color.

ACTIVE TIME: 15 MINUTES **TOTAL TIME:** 15 MINUTES, PLUS CHILLING **MAKES:** 4 SERVINGS

1   (16-ounce) package firm tofu, drained

¼   cup Vegan Mayonnaise (page 29)

1   tablespoon sweet pickle relish

2   teaspoons soy milk

¾   teaspoon Dijon mustard

salt

½   teaspoon turmeric

2   small stalks celery, thinly sliced

8   slices whole-grain bread

1   head Boston lettuce

2   small ripe tomatoes (4 ounces each), sliced

1 In a medium bowl, with a fork, mix the tofu
with the mayonnaise, pickle relish, soy milk,
mustard, ½ teaspoon salt, and turmeric until the
tofu breaks down into small pieces the size of
peas. Stir in the celery. Cover and refrigerate to
allow flavors to blend or until ready to serve.

2 To serve, top 4 bread slices with the tofu
mixture and arrange the lettuce leaves and
tomato slices on top; cover with the remaining
bread slices.

EACH SERVING: ABOUT 305 CALORIES, 19G PROTEIN,
31G CARBOHYDRATE, 12G TOTAL FAT (2G SATURATED),
6G FIBER, 696MG SODIUM

TIP

You can use store-bought vegan mayonnaise,
or try our easy recipe on page 29.

Falafel WRAPS

Serve these small Middle Eastern bean patties
in pita pockets with lettuce, tomatoes, cucumbers, and tangy,
nondairy yogurt. For photo, see page 26.

For photo, see page 26.

ACTIVE TIME: 10 MINUTES   **TOTAL TIME:** 25 MINUTES   **MAKES:** 4 SERVINGS

4   green onions, cut into ½-inch pieces

2   garlic cloves, each cut in half

½   cup packed fresh Italian parsley leaves

2   teaspoons dried mint

1   (15- to 19-ounce) can garbanzo beans, drained and rinsed

½   cup plain dried bread crumbs

1   teaspoon ground coriander

1   teaspoon ground cumin

1   teaspoon baking powder

salt

¼   teaspoon cayenne pepper

¼   teaspoon ground allspice

olive oil nonstick cooking spray

4   (6- to 7-inch) whole wheat pita breads

sliced romaine lettuce, sliced ripe tomatoes, sliced cucumber, sliced red onion, nondairy plain yogurt (optional), for serving

1 In a food processor with knife blade attached, finely chop the green onions, garlic, parsley leaves, and mint. Add the beans, bread crumbs, coriander, cumin, baking powder, ½ teaspoon salt, cayenne, and allspice; blend until a coarse puree forms.

2 With your hands, shape the bean mixture by scant ½ cups into eight 3-inch round patties and place on a sheet of waxed paper. Coat both sides of the patties with cooking spray.

3 Heat a nonstick 10-inch skillet on medium-high until hot. Add half of the patties and cook until they're dark golden brown, about 8 minutes, turning over once. Transfer the patties to paper towels to drain. Repeat with remaining patties.

4 Cut off the top third of each pita to form a pocket. Place two warm patties in each pita. Serve with your choice of accompaniments.

EACH SERVING: ABOUT 365 CALORIES, 14G PROTEIN 68G CARBOHYDRATE, 5G TOTAL FAT (1G SATURATED), 10G FIBER, 1,015MG SODIUM

HEALTHY
Club Sandwiches

This carrot, sprout, and bean spread combo will
delight your palate and satisfy your hunger.

ACTIVE TIME: 25 MINUTES   **TOTAL TIME:** 25 MINUTES   **MAKES:** 4 SERVINGS

olive oil

2   teaspoons, plus 1 tablespoon fresh
    lemon juice

1   teaspoon honey or agave nectar

ground black pepper

3   carrots, peeled and shredded (about 1 cup)

2   cups alfalfa sprouts

1   garlic clove, finely chopped

½   teaspoon ground cumin

pinch cayenne pepper

1   (15- to 19-ounce) can garbanzo beans,
    drained and rinsed

8   slices multigrain bread, lightly toasted

1   large ripe tomato (10 to 12 ounces),
    thinly sliced

1   bunch watercress (4 ounces), tough
    stems trimmed

1 In a medium bowl, stir 1 tablespoon oil,
2 teaspoons lemon juice, honey or agave nectar,
and ⅛ teaspoon pepper until mixed. Add the
carrots and alfalfa sprouts; toss until mixed and
evenly coated with dressing.

2 In a 2-quart saucepan, heat 1 tablespoon oil
over medium heat. Add the garlic, cumin, and
cayenne and cook until very fragrant. Stir in the
garbanzo beans and remove from heat. Add the
remaining 1 tablespoon lemon juice and
1 tablespoon water; mash to a coarse puree.

3 Spread the bean mixture on 8 toast slices.
Place the tomato slices and watercress over
4 slices. Top with the alfalfa-sprout mixture.
Cover with the 4 remaining toast slices, placing
the garbanzo-topped sides onto the filling.

EACH SERVING: ABOUT 380 CALORIES, 14G PROTEIN,
57G CARBOHYDRATE, 12G TOTAL FAT (2G SATURATED),
17G FIBER, 545MG SODIUM

TIP

Many vegans consider honey off-limits
because it is a by-product of bees (just as
milk is a by-product of cows). Agave nectar
is a natural sweetener derived from cactuses
that's a great substitute.

Herb-Roasted Root Vegetables
(page 53)

3 Salads

Salads are terrific building blocks for vegan meals. Whether you prepare a hearty main-dish salad featuring grains or pasta or a selection of side-dish salads, you can count on salads to help you create meals that are nutritious and delicious. Although we usually think of salads as a combination of vegetables tossed with greens, this chapter encourages you to expand your definition. Pasta, grains, or beans can each serve as the foundation of a satisfying salad, as our recipes for Lentil & Spinach Salad, Garlic Greens & Pumpernickel Panzanella, and Hearty Kale & Bean Salad attest. In fact, building a salad around whole grains is a particularly smart way to create robust main dishes. Pair your grain of choice with a rainbow of fresh vegetables, greens, and fruit, and you have a meal that's bursting with antioxidant goodness.

Hearty Kale &
BEAN SALAD

This filling, vegetarian salad is substantial enough
to serve as a main dish.

ACTIVE TIME: 5 MINUTES   TOTAL TIME: 5 MINUTES   MAKES: 4 SERVINGS

10   ounces Tuscan kale

2   cups Brussels sprouts, thinly sliced

3   tablespoons lemon juice

1   garlic clove

salt

ground black pepper

extra-virgin olive oil

1   (15-ounce) can cannellini beans

⅓   cup toasted walnuts

1   cup vegan Parmesan, (such as Go Veggie)

toast, for serving (optional)

1 In a large serving bowl, mix the kale and
Brussels sprouts.
2 In a small bowl, whisk the lemon juice, garlic,
and ¼ teaspoon each of salt and pepper. Whisk
in 3 tablespoons oil. Toss the dressing with the
kale mixture. Add the cannellini beans, toasted
walnuts, and Parmesan, and toss again. Serve
with toast, if you like.

EACH SERVING: ABOUT 455 CALORIES, 25G PROTEIN,
33G CARBOHYDRATE, 27G TOTAL FAT (8G SATURATED),
13G FIBER, 780MG SODIUM

Lentil & Spinach
SALAD

If you're concerned about eating enough protein
and dietary fiber, this dish serves both in a single bowl.

ACTIVE TIME: 25 MINUTES   **TOTAL TIME:** 40 MINUTES   **MAKES:** 12 SERVINGS

1½ cups lentils

2   carrots, peeled and cut into ¼-inch pieces

2   Golden Delicious apples, cored and cut into
       ¼-inch pieces

3   lemons

olive oil

¼   cup balsamic vinegar

1½ teaspoons sugar

salt

ground black pepper

2   (10-ounce) packages spinach, tough stems
       trimmed

chopped fresh parsley, for garnish

1 Rinse the lentils under cold running water
and discard any stones or shriveled beans. In
a 4-quart saucepan, combine the lentils and 8
cups water; heat to boiling over high heat. Stir in
the carrots and apples; heat to boiling. Reduce
the heat to low and simmer until the lentils are
tender, 15 to 20 minutes; drain.

2 Meanwhile, from lemons, grate 2 teaspoons
peel and squeeze ¼ cup juice. In a small bowl,
with a wire whisk or fork, combine 1/3 cup oil,
vinegar, sugar, 1½ teaspoons salt, 3/4 teaspoon
pepper, lemon juice, and lemon peel.

3 To serve, in a large bowl, toss the spinach with
1 cup dressing. Stir the remaining dressing into
the lentil mixture. Place the spinach leaves on
salad plates and top with the lentils. Sprinkle
with parsley.

EACH SERVING: ABOUT 165 CALORIES, 8G PROTEIN,
20G CARBOHYDRATE, 6G TOTAL FAT (1G SATURATED),
12G FIBER, 345MG SODIUM

TIP

To store washed greens, layer the leaves
between barely dampened paper towels
and place in a perforated plastic vegetable
bag (sold next to the sandwich bags in the
supermarket) or in a zip-tight plastic bag
with a few holes poked in it. (Seal the bag
loosely.) Leafy greens should stay fresh in
the crisper for up to 5 days.

CRUNCHY BULGUR
Lettuce Cups

Whip up these handheld lettuce cups
for a fun and healthy meal.

ACTIVE TIME: 10 MINUTES   TOTAL TIME: 20 MINUTES   MAKES: 6 SERVINGS

extra-virgin olive oil

1   large shallot, finely chopped

6   ounces shiitake mushrooms, stemmed
    and sliced

3   tablespoons champagne vinegar

2   cups cooked bulgur

¼   cup finely chopped mint

kosher salt

small lettuce cups

½   cup roasted salted almonds, chopped,
    for garnish

1 In a 10-inch skillet, heat 2 tablespoons olive
oil on medium. Add the shallot and cook for
3 minutes, stirring. Add the mushrooms and cook
for 5 minutes more. Add the champagne vinegar
and remove from heat, scraping up browned bits.
2 Toss with the bulgur, mint, 2 tablespoons olive
oil, and 1 teaspoon salt. Spoon into lettuce cups.
Top with chopped almonds and serve.

EACH SERVING: ABOUT 220 CALORIES, 6G PROTEIN,
18G CARBOHYDRATE, 15G TOTAL FAT (2G SATURATED),
6G FIBER, 395MG SODIUM

GARLIC GREENS & PUMPERNICKEL
Panzanella

Toasted bread and zesty dressing
bring this green salad to another level.

ACTIVE TIME: 25 MINUTES   **TOTAL TIME:** 35 MINUTES   **MAKES:** 6 SERVINGS

1   pound asparagus, trimmed and cut into
    1-inch lengths

1   bunch green onions, cut into 1-inch
    lengths

extra-virgin olive oil

salt

6   cups pumpernickel bread, cut into
    ¼-inch cubes

2   tablespoons fresh lemon juice

1   tablespoon white wine vinegar

1   tablespoon spicy brown mustard

1   tablespoon prepared horseradish

¼   cup chopped fresh dill

4   cups arugula

½   bunch watermelon radishes or regular
    radishes, trimmed and thinly sliced

1   Arrange two oven racks in the upper and
lower thirds of your oven. Preheat the oven to
450°F. On a large rimmed baking sheet, toss the
asparagus, green onions, 2 teaspoons olive oil,
and ¼ teaspoon salt; spread in a single layer.
Bake on the lower rack until the vegetables are
browned and tender, 15 minutes. On another
large rimmed baking sheet, arrange the bread in
a single layer. Bake on the upper rack until crisp
and dry, stirring once; 10 to 12 minutes.

2   Meanwhile, in a large bowl, whisk 2 tablespoons
oil with lemon juice, vinegar, mustard,
horseradish, and ½ teaspoon salt; stir in the dill.

3   Toss the bread cubes with the vinaigrette in
a bowl; add the roasted vegetables, arugula, and
radishes; toss until well-combined.

EACH SERVING: ABOUT 330 CALORIES, 11G PROTEIN,
51G CARBOHYDRATE, 10G TOTAL FAT (1G SATURATED),
9G FIBER, 870MG SODIUM

Beet, Mushroom &
AVOCADO SALAD

This heart-healthy salad is loaded with antioxidants, fiber-filled vegetables, and healthy unsaturated fats (hello, avocado!).

ACTIVE TIME: 10 MINUTES **TOTAL TIME:** 30 MINUTES **MAKES:** 4 SERVINGS

4   medium portobello mushroom caps

nonstick cooking spray

salt

¼   cup lemon juice

extra-virgin olive oil

1   small shallot, finely chopped

ground black pepper

5   ounces baby kale

8   ounces precooked beets, chopped

2   ripe avocados, thinly sliced

2   sheets matzo, crushed into bite-size pieces

1 On a large rimmed baking sheet, spray the portobello mushroom caps with nonstick cooking spray and sprinkle with ½ teaspoon salt; roast at 450°F for 20 minutes or until tender.

2 Whisk the lemon juice, 3 tablespoons oil, shallot, and ¼ teaspoon each salt and pepper; toss half of the mixture with the baby kale and beets. Divide among serving plates. Top with the avocados, matzo, and mushrooms, thinly sliced. Serve with the remaining dressing on the side.

EACH SERVING: ABOUT 370 CALORIES, 7G PROTEIN, 32G CARBOHYDRATE, 26G TOTAL FAT (4G SATURATED), 11G FIBER, 490MG SODIUM

CUCUMBER, ROASTED BEET
& Pistachio Salad

Beets are a great source of essential nutrients,
including B vitamins, iron, manganese, copper, and potassium.

ACTIVE TIME: 30 MINUTES   **TOTAL TIME:** 1 HOUR   **MAKES:** 8 SERVINGS

3   pounds medium beets, trimmed,
    scrubbed and very thinly sliced

olive oil

salt

1   large seedless cucumber, thinly sliced

2   tablespoons sherry vinegar

toasted sesame oil

ground black pepper

½   cup roasted salted pistachios, shelled
    and chopped, for garnish

1 Preheat your oven to 450°F. Toss the beets
with 3 tablespoons olive oil and ¼ teaspoon salt;
spread out in single layers on 2 large rimmed
baking sheets. Roast for 30 minutes or until
tender, switching pans on racks halfway through.
Let cool.

2 Meanwhile, in a medium bowl, toss the
cucumber with ¼ teaspoon salt; transfer to a
colander to drain.

3 Toss the cucumber with vinegar, 1 tablespoon
sesame oil, and ¼ teaspoon pepper until well
coated; fold in the beets. Transfer to a serving
platter. Top with pistachios.

EACH SERVING: ABOUT 155 CALORIES, 4G PROTEIN,
14G CARBOHYDRATE, 11G TOTAL FAT (1G SATURATED),
4G FIBER, 270MG SODIUM

Lentil Salad
WITH ROASTED VEGGIES

Roasted vegetables and lentils make this colorful salad
into a healthy, filling meal.

ACTIVE TIME: 30 MINUTES   **TOTAL TIME:** 40 MINUTES   **MAKES:** 4 SERVINGS

2 cups dried green lentils

1 bunch asparagus

1 small red pepper

1 small red onion

extra-virgin olive oil

¾ teaspoon ground cumin

salt

ground black pepper

¼ cup fresh lime juice

⅓ cup finely chopped fresh mint leaves

6 cups mixed greens

1 Preheat your oven to 450°F. In a 4-quart covered saucepan, heat 6 cups of water to a boil on high. Stir in the lentils. Reduce the heat to maintain a simmer. Simmer while covered, for 25 to 30 minutes or until tender, stirring occasionally. Drain well.

2 Meanwhile, in a large jelly-roll pan, toss the asparagus, red pepper, and onion with 1 tablespoon oil, ½ teaspoon cumin, and ¼ teaspoon each of salt and pepper. Roast for 18 to 20 minutes or until tender, stirring halfway through.

3 In a large bowl, whisk together the lime juice, mint, 3 tablespoons of oil, the remaining ¼ teaspoon cumin, and ¼ teaspoon each of salt and pepper. Add the hot lentils and vegetables to the dressing and toss until well coated. Divide the greens among serving plates. Top with the lentil mixture.

EACH SERVING: ABOUT 505 CALORIES, 26G PROTEIN, 63G CARBOHYDRATE, 19G TOTAL FAT (4G SATURATED), 17G FIBER, 375MG SODIUM

Adding Proteins to Salads

There are plenty of satisfying ways to
up the protein in vegan salads.

BEANS AND LEGUMES

Beans are a vegan's best friend. A serving
of beans—canned or home-cooked—
adds not only protein but fiber and lots
of vitamins, too. Black, pinto, kidney,
cannellini, and garbanzo beans are obvious
choices, but lentils, Great Northern beans,
adzuki, edamame, and mung beans will
all add color, texture, and—yes—protein to
greens, mixed vegetables, or pasta salads.

NUTS AND SEEDS

Sprinkling your salads with nuts or seeds is
a glorious way to add protein and heart-
healthy fats. Don't limit yourself to walnuts
and sliced almonds—consider hazelnuts,
pecans, sesame seeds, or pumpkin seeds.
Toasting nuts in the oven for 10 minutes or
on the stovetop for 5 minutes will add flavor
and fragrance to your salad du jour.

SOY PRODUCTS

Grilled or baked tofu slices or sautéed
tempeh are great protein-rich additions to
salads, especially if you marinate them in a
little dressing before cooking. You can also
find soy chicken and beef strips at your
supermarket or health-food store—flavored
or not—that will turn your garden-variety
salad into a thing of beauty.

TIP

To toast almonds, preheat your oven
to 350°F. Spread nuts in a single layer
on a sheet pan and bake, stirring
occasionally, until lightly browned
and fragrant, about 10 minutes.

Sweet Potato Cakes
WITH KALE & BEAN SALAD

These hearty sweet potato cakes are balanced with
a bright and earthy salad featuring two types of legumes.
For photo, see page 6.

ACTIVE TIME: 15 MINUTES   **TOTAL TIME:** 40 MINUTES   **MAKES:** 4 SERVINGS

nonstick cooking spray

3   sweet potatoes, peeled and shredded

2   green onions, thinly sliced

salt

ground black pepper

¼   cup Vegan Mayonnaise (page 29)

2   tablespoons lime juice

1   tablespoon soy sauce

5   ounces baby kale

2   (15-ounce) cans no-salt-added black beans,
     drained and rinsed

2   cups shelled frozen edamame

1 Preheat your oven to 450°F. Spray a cookie
sheet with cooking spray. In a large bowl, toss the
sweet potatoes, green onions, and ¼ teaspoon
each salt and pepper. With a ¼-cup measure,
scoop the packed sweet potatoes onto a pan to
form 12 mounds, 2 inches apart. Flatten slightly.
Spray the tops with cooking spray. Bake for 25
minutes or until browned at the edges.

2 In a large bowl, whisk the Vegan Mayonnaise,
lime juice, and soy sauce. When the cakes are
cooked, add the baby kale, black beans, and
edamame to the dressing. Toss until coated.

3 Serve cakes over salad.

EACH SERVING: ABOUT 375 CALORIES, 21G PROTEIN,
56G CARBOHYDRATE, 9G TOTAL FAT (1G SATURATED),
16G FIBER, 530 MG SODIUM

HERB-ROASTED
Root Vegetables

Rich in color and flavor, these root veggies,
dressed in thyme and parsley, are the perfect spring side dish.
For photo, see page 38.

ACTIVE TIME: 15 MINUTES   **TOTAL TIME:** 1 HOUR   **MAKES:** 10 SERVINGS

1½ pounds mixed baby potatoes, cut
     into halves

1   pound baby carrots, cut into halves

salt

1   bunch radishes, trimmed, cut into halves

olive oil

1   tablespoon chopped fresh thyme

ground black pepper

¼   cup fresh parsley, finely chopped

1 Preheat your oven to 450°F. In a 7-quart
saucepot, cover the potatoes and carrots with
cold water; add 1 tablespoon salt. Cover and heat
to boiling on high. Reduce the heat to maintain
a simmer; cook for 7 minutes. Drain well and
return to the pot.

2 Toss the potatoes, carrots, and radishes with
3 tablespoons oil, thyme, and ¼ teaspoon each
salt and pepper; arrange in a single layer on a
large rimmed baking sheet. Roast for 20 minutes
or until the vegetables are browned and tender.

3 Remove from the oven; sprinkle vegetables
with parsley.

EACH SERVING: ABOUT 110 CALORIES, 2G PROTEIN,
16G CARBOHYDRATE, 4G TOTAL FAT (1G SATURATED),
2G FIBER, 170MG SODIUM

Roasted Vegetable Penne
(page 63)

4 | Noodles

Who can live without noodles? Not us! We've gathered a collection of our favorite vegan-friendly pasta and noodle dishes, ranging from tempting Soba Noodles Primavera with Miso to an easy Middle Eastern Garbanzo Beans & Macaroni. Pasta is a great playground for vegetables: throw together our Roasted Veggie Penne or Veggie Lo Mein, and you'll see! Pasta dinners are also another opportunity to incorporate whole grains in your family's diet. In fact, a whole-grain makeover for your favorite pasta dishes is as simple as buying whole-grain or 100 percent whole wheat pasta instead of egg- or semolina-based pastas. Just be sure to read the labels closely when purchasing whole-grain pastas. For example, a pasta may proclaim itself multigrain, but if you read the label, you might find that semolina, a refined flour, is the number-one ingredient.

VEGGIE **Lo Mein**

This spin on a Chinese takeout classic is crazy healthy
with edamame that packs protein, fiber, and
essential vitamins and minerals.

ACTIVE TIME: 20 MINUTES   **TOTAL TIME:** 20 MINUTES   **MAKES:** 4 SERVINGS

1   (8-ounce) package whole-grain spaghetti

1   (10-ounce) package frozen chopped broccoli

1½ cups frozen shelled edamame

2   cups shredded carrots

1   (10-ounce) package baby spinach

toasted sesame oil

1   large onion, thinly sliced

2   teaspoons fresh ginger, grated and peeled

¼   cup, plus 1 teaspoon low-sodium soy sauce

2   tablespoons balsamic vinegar

1   cup crumbled firm tofu

1 Cook the spaghetti in a large pot of boiling
water as the package label directs. Just before
draining, add the broccoli, edamame, carrots,
and spinach. Drain well; set aside.

2 In the same pot, heat 2 tablespoons oil on
medium-high. Add the onion; cook for 5 minutes.
Add the ginger, soy sauce, and balsamic vinegar.
Cook for 1 minute. Stir in tofu and cook for
1 minute. Add the noodle mixture; cook, tossing,
for 2 minutes or until heated through.

EACH SERVING: ABOUT 460 CALORIES, 25G PROTEIN,
63G CARBOHYDRATE, 15G TOTAL FAT (3G SATURATED),
15G FIBER, 785MG SODIUM

Soba Noodles
WITH GRILLED TOFU

Soba noodles are made from buckwheat flour
and are gluten-free and a good source of protein and fiber.

ACTIVE TIME: 20 MINUTES   **TOTAL TIME:** 30 MINUTES   **MAKES:** 4 SERVINGS

1   (12-ounce) package extra-firm tofu

kosher salt

ground black pepper

8   ounces soba noodles

5   ounces baby spinach

3   tablespoons low-sodium soy sauce

1   tablespoon lime juice

6   radishes, thinly sliced

¼   cup peanuts, chopped, for garnish

1 Cut the tofu into ½-inch-thick slices and press dry with paper towels. Season with salt and pepper. Grill on medium-high for 10 to 15 minutes while covered, turning once. Cut into bite-size pieces.

2 Meanwhile, cook the soba noodles according to package directions. Place the baby spinach in a colander in the sink; drain the hot noodles directly over the spinach. Rinse with cold water and drain well. Toss with the soy sauce, lime juice, radishes, and grilled tofu. Top with peanuts.

EACH SERVING: ABOUT 360 CALORIES, 18G PROTEIN, 51G CARBOHYDRATE, 10G TOTAL FAT (1G SATURATED), 6G FIBER, 775 MG SODIUM

TOFU **Pad Thai**

Pad thai, Thailand's popular stir-fried noodle dish, is usually prepared with shrimp and scrambled eggs. Here we load up on green veggies and substitute tofu cubes for the eggs.

ACTIVE TIME: 30 MINUTES   TOTAL TIME: 30 MINUTES, PLUS SOAKING   MAKES: 4 SERVINGS

8   ounces rice noodles (rice vermicelli) or angel-hair pasta

¼   cup fresh lime juice

3   tablespoons soy sauce

2   tablespoons sugar

Asian chili oil

2   large garlic cloves, crushed with press

1   pound firm tofu, drained and cut into ½-inch pieces

4   cups shredded cabbage

⅓   cup unsalted roasted peanuts, coarsely chopped

2   green onions, thinly sliced, for garnish

1 In a large bowl, soak the rice noodles in enough very hot water to cover, 25 minutes. (If using angel-hair pasta, break the pasta in half and cook as the package label directs; rinse under cold water to stop the cooking; drain.)

2 Meanwhile, in a small bowl, combine the lime juice, soy sauce, sugar, and 2 tablespoons water.

3 In a nonstick 12-inch skillet, heat 1½ to 2 teaspoons oil over medium-high heat until hot. Stir in the garlic; cook for 30 seconds. Add the tofu and cook for 1 minute or just until heated through, stirring frequently.

4 Drain the rice noodles. Add the noodles or angel-hair pasta to the skillet and cook for 2 minutes, stirring constantly. Add the soy sauce mixture, cabbage, and peanuts; cook for 1 minute.

5 Transfer the pad thai to bowls. Top with green onions.

EACH SERVING: ABOUT 435 CALORIES, 15G PROTEIN, 66G CARBOHYDRATE, 13G TOTAL FAT (1.5G SATURATED), 4G FIBER, 706MG SODIUM

Sesame NOODLES

A peanut butter-and-sesame dressing spiked with
orange juice makes this Chinese restaurant-style pasta
a favorite with kids as well as adults.

ACTIVE TIME: 15 MINUTES   TOTAL TIME: 30 MINUTES   MAKES: 6 SERVINGS

1   (16-ounce) package spaghetti

1   cup fresh orange juice

¼   cup seasoned rice vinegar

¼   cup soy sauce

¼   cup creamy peanut butter

Asian sesame oil

1   tablespoon grated, peeled fresh ginger

2   teaspoons sugar

¼   teaspoon crushed red pepper

1   (10-ounce) package shredded carrots
     (about 3½ cups)

3   Kirby cucumbers (about 4 ounces each),
     unpeeled and cut into 2 x ¼-inch matchstick
     strips

2   green onions, trimmed and thinly sliced

2   tablespoons sesame seeds, toasted
     (optional)

green onions, chopped, for garnish

1 In a large saucepot, cook the pasta as the package label directs, but do not add salt to the water.

2 Meanwhile, in a medium bowl, with a wire whisk or fork, mix the orange juice, vinegar, soy sauce, peanut butter, 1 tablespoon oil, ginger, sugar, and crushed red pepper until blended; set aside.

3 Place the carrots in a colander; drain the pasta over the carrots. In a warm serving bowl, toss the pasta mixture, cucumbers, and sliced green onions with the peanut sauce. If you like, sprinkle the pasta with sesame seeds. Garnish with green onions.

EACH SERVING: ABOUT 445 CALORIES, 15G PROTEIN, 7G CARBOHYDRATE, 9G TOTAL FAT (2G SATURATED), 5G FIBER, 1,125MG SODIUM

Soba Noodles Primavera
WITH MISO

This quick and easy Asian-inspired pasta primavera uses soba noodles and miso for a nutritional boost.

ACTIVE TIME: 20 MINUTES   **TOTAL TIME:** 40 MINUTES   **MAKES:** 4 SERVINGS

1   (16-ounce) package extra-firm tofu, drained and patted dry

1   (8-ounce) package soba noodles

olive oil

1   medium red pepper (4 to 6 ounces), thinly sliced

1   large onion (12 ounces), sliced

2   garlic cloves, crushed with press

1   tablespoon grated, peeled fresh ginger

¼   teaspoon crushed red pepper

1   (16-ounce) package broccoli florets, cut into 1½-inch pieces

1   (10-ounce) package shredded carrots

¼   cup red (dark) miso paste

2   green onions, thinly sliced

1   Cut the tofu in half horizontally. Cut each half into 1-inch pieces; set aside.

2   In a large saucepot, prepare the noodles as the package label directs.

3   Meanwhile, in a nonstick 5- to 6-quart Dutch oven, heat 1 tablespoon oil over medium-high heat until hot. Add the red pepper and onion; cook until golden, about 10 minutes, stirring occasionally. Add the garlic, ginger, crushed red pepper, and tofu; cook for 1 minute, stirring. Add the broccoli, carrots, and ¼ cup water; heat to boiling over medium-high heat. Reduce heat to medium; cover and cook until the vegetables are tender, about 7 minutes.

4   When the noodles have cooked to your desired doneness, drain, reserving ¾ cup cooking water. Return the noodles to the saucepot.

5   With a wire whisk, mix the miso paste into the reserved noodle cooking water until blended.

6   To serve, toss the noodles with the tofu mixture, green onions, and miso paste mixture.

EACH SERVING: ABOUT 455 CALORIES, 26G PROTEIN, 68G CARBOHYDRATE, 11G TOTAL FAT (2G SATURATED), 11G FIBER, 1,290MG SODIUM

Roasted Veggie
PENNE

A whole-grain pasta, plus loads of veggies,
makes a slimming meal. For photo, see page 54.

ACTIVE TIME: 20 MINUTES   **TOTAL TIME:** 40 MINUTES   **MAKES:** 4 SERVINGS

2	medium zucchini
2	medium red or yellow peppers
3	cups broccoli florets
1	medium red onion
2	garlic cloves
	extra-virgin olive oil
	salt
12	ounces whole-grain penne
1	(28-ounce) can crushed tomatoes
¼	cup fresh basil leaves
½	teaspoon crushed red pepper

1 Preheat your oven to 450°F. Heat a large pot of salted water to boil on high.

2 In a large bowl, combine zucchini, peppers, broccoli, onion, garlic, and 1 tablespoon oil. Divide among two 18 x 12-inch jelly-roll pans. Sprinkle with ½ teaspoon salt. Roast for 15 to 20 minutes or until browned and tender, stir once.

3 While the vegetables cook, add the penne to the boiling water. Cook as the package label directs. Reserve ½ cup cooking water. Drain the pasta and return it to the pot.

4 To the pasta, add the tomatoes, basil, crushed red pepper, roasted vegetable mixture, and ⅛ teaspoon salt. Stir to combine, adding cooking water if necessary. Cook on medium for 2 minutes.

EACH SERVING: ABOUT 500 CALORIES, 20G PROTEIN, 85G CARBOHYDRATE, 10G TOTAL FAT (3G SATURATED), 14G FIBER, 895MG SODIUM

Creamy Vegan Linguine
WITH WILD MUSHROOMS

You don't need cream for a truly decadent pasta sauce.
Mushrooms add an earthy flavor to a satisfying dish.

ACTIVE TIME: 10 MINUTES   **TOTAL TIME:** 20 MINUTES   **MAKES:** 6 SERVINGS

1   pound linguine or fettuccine

olive oil

12   ounces mixed mushrooms, thinly sliced

3   garlic cloves, finely chopped

¼   cup nutritional yeast

salt

ground black pepper

2   green onions, thinly sliced on an angle,
for garnish

1 Cook the linguine as the package label directs, reserving ¾ cup pasta cooking water before draining. Return the drained linguine to the pot.
2 Meanwhile, in a 12-inch skillet, heat 6 tablespoons oil on medium-high heat. Add the mushrooms and garlic; cook for 5 minutes or until mushrooms are browned and tender, stirring. Transfer to the pot with the cooked drained linguine, along with the nutritional yeast, reserved cooking water, ½ teaspoon salt, and ¾ teaspoon pepper. Toss until well combined. Garnish with green onions.

EACH SERVING: ABOUT 430 CALORIES, 15G PROTEIN, 62G CARBOHYDRATE, 15G TOTAL FAT (2G SATURATED), 5G FIBER, 175MG SODIUM

TIP

Nutritional yeast, or nooch, is essential in a vegan kitchen. Nutritional yeast is nutty, tasty, versatile, and packed with B vitamins, which help support the immune and nervous systems.

Risotto
PUTTANESCA

Although a labor of love,
this risotto dish will leave you full and satisfied.

ACTIVE TIME: 35 MINUTES TOTAL TIME: 35 MINUTES MAKES: 8 SERVINGS

1   quart low-sodium vegetable broth

olive oil

1   medium onion, finely chopped

1   pound Arborio or Carnaroli rice

1   (6-ounce) can tomato paste

1   cup Kalamata olives, pitted and chopped

¼   cup fresh parsley, chopped

3   tablespoons capers, drained

2   tablespoons vegan margarine or butter,
     room temperature (such as Earth Balance)

salt

ground black pepper

1 In a 3-quart saucepan, combine the broth with 7 cups water; cover and heat to simmering on high. Reduce heat to low.

2 In a 5- to 6-quart saucepot, heat 2 tablespoons oil over medium heat. Add the onion; cook for 5 minutes or until translucent, stirring occasionally. Add the rice; cook for 1 minute, stirring. Add 2 ladlefuls of broth to the rice; stir until most of the liquid is absorbed before adding another ladleful. Reduce the heat to medium-low. Continue adding broth and stirring until about 1 cup of broth remains in the saucepan; whisk the tomato paste into the broth. Add this tomato broth to the rice, stirring until the liquid is absorbed and the rice is tender.

3 Gently fold the olives, parsley, capers, margarine, 1 teaspoon salt, and ½ teaspoon pepper into rice. Serve risotto immediately.

EACH SERVING: ABOUT 445 CALORIES, 11G PROTEIN, 69G CARBOHYDRATE, 15G TOTAL FAT (4G SATURATED), 5G FIBER, 825MG SODIUM

TIP

We made a big batch of this recipe to produce leftovers for risotto cakes! Use ¼ cup of risotto to form 2-inch patties, coat in Japanese bread crumbs, and bake in a 475°F oven for 15 minutes. Serve with a simple side salad.

SWEET & TANGY
Pasta Salad

Amp up your BBQ with this next-level pasta salad.

ACTIVE TIME: 10 MINUTES   **TOTAL TIME:** 10 MINUTES   **MAKES:** 4 SERVINGS

CREAMY BALSAMIC DRESSING

1   cup reduced-calorie mayo

½   cup balsamic vinegar

olive oil

2   garlic cloves, crushed

kosher salt

ground black pepper

SALAD

1   (1-pound) box of whole-grain rotini, cooked, slightly cooled

3   celery stalk, thinly sliced

3   carrots, shredded

1   red pepper, chopped

1   (5-ounce) package arugula

2   (15-ounce) cans cannellini beans, drained and rinsed

1 Make the Creamy Balsamic Dressing: In a bowl, with a fork, combine the mayo, balsamic vinegar, ¼ cup oil, garlic, salt, and pepper.

2 Make the Salad: Toss the balsamic dressing with the rotini, celery, carrots, red pepper, arugula, and cannellini beans.

EACH SERVING: ABOUT 290 CALORIES, 11G PROTEIN, 46G CARBOHYDRATE, 8G TOTAL FAT (1G SATURATED), 9G FIBER, 283MG SODIUM

TIP

If you have extra dressing, it will keep in your fridge for up to 3 weeks.

Polenta
WITH SPICY EGGPLANT SAUCE

A great dinner you can whip up after you get home from work:
Polenta cooks in the microwave oven with minimal attention
while you prepare a quick skillet sauce.

ACTIVE TIME: 15 MINUTES **TOTAL TIME:** 40 MINUTES **MAKES:** 4 SERVINGS

olive oil

1 medium onion, finely chopped

2 small eggplants (about 1 pound each),
cut into 1-inch chunks

1 garlic clove, crushed

¼ teaspoon crushed red pepper

1 (28-ounce) can crushed tomatoes

salt

2 cups plain soy milk

1½ cups yellow cornmeal

nondairy Parmesan, grated, and parsley
sprigs, for garnish (optional)

1 In a nonstick 12-inch skillet, heat 1 tablespoon oil over medium heat. Add the onion and cook for 5 minutes, stirring occasionally. Increase heat to medium-high; add the eggplant and cook for 8 minutes or until golden and tender, stirring occasionally. Add the garlic and crushed red pepper and cook for 1 minute, stirring. Add the tomatoes, ½ teaspoon salt, and ½ cup water; heat to boiling. Reduce heat to low; cover and simmer 10 minutes, stirring occasionally.

2 Meanwhile, in a deep 4-quart microwave-safe bowl or casserole dish, combine the milk, cornmeal, 1 teaspoon salt, and 4½ cups water. Cook in microwave oven on High for 15 to 20 minutes, until thickened. After the first 5 minutes of cooking, whisk vigorously until smooth (mixture will be lumpy at first); do so twice more during the remaining cooking time.

3 To serve, spoon the polenta into 4 bowls; top with the eggplant sauce. Garnish each serving with some grated Parmesan and a parsley sprig, if you like.

EACH SERVING: ABOUT 380 CALORIES, 13G PROTEIN, 71G CARBOHYDRATE, 6G TOTAL FAT (2G SATURATED), 12G FIBER, 1,235MG SODIUM

Macaroni &
"CHEESE"

Here's everyone's favorite comfort food, vegan style.

ACTIVE TIME: 5 MINUTES TOTAL TIME: 15 MINUTES MAKES: 8 SERVINGS

10 to 12 ounces elbow macaroni

1 (12-ounce) package silken tofu

salt

2 tablespoons vegan stick margarine or butter

1½ cups packed shredded soy Cheddar cheese

½ cup plain unsweetened soy milk or almond milk

1 Cook the macaroni as the package label directs, but do not add salt to water. Drain and set aside.

2 Drain the tofu, and puree in a food processor until completely smooth. Pour into a medium saucepan and add ½ teaspoon salt, vegan margarine, soy Cheddar, and soy milk. Bring to a simmer over low heat, stirring frequently. Once hot, add the macaroni and stir until heated through.

EACH SERVING: ABOUT 265 CALORIES, 14G PROTEIN, 33G CARBOHYDRATE, 7G TOTAL FAT (1G SATURATED), 2G FIBER, 478MG SODIUM

The Skinny on Soy Cheese

If eliminating cheese from your diet feels like a sacrifice, take heart. Soy versions of many cheeses are now available, including cream cheese, Cheddar, grated Parmesan, Monterey Jack, and even feta. If you can't locate them at your local supermarket, check a health-food store or surf the web for online sources. Some versions are more convincing than others and flavor varies from brand to brand, so some experimentation is needed in order to find cheese substitutions you like. Vegan options typically don't melt as nicely as dairy cheese, but if you're hankering for cheese, you can find options that satisfy your craving.

MIDDLE EASTERN
Garbanzo Beans & Macaroni

A flavorful entrée based on pantry staples—canned garbanzo beans and crushed tomatoes—tossed with pasta.

ACTIVE TIME: 10 MINUTES · **TOTAL TIME:** 35 MINUTES · **MAKES:** 6 SERVINGS

12 ounces macaroni twists or elbow macaroni

olive oil

1 tablespoon vegan stick margarine or butter

1 large onion (12 ounces), cut into ¼-inch pieces

2 garlic cloves, crushed

salt

1 teaspoon ground cumin

¾ teaspoon ground coriander

¼ teaspoon ground allspice

ground black pepper

1 (28-ounce) can crushed tomatoes

1 (15- to 19-ounce) can garbanzo beans, drained and rinsed

¼ cup loosely packed fresh parsley leaves, chopped

parsley sprigs, for garnish

1 In a large saucepot, cook the pasta as the package label directs.

2 Meanwhile, in a nonstick 12-inch skillet, heat 1 tablespoon oil with margarine over medium heat until hot and melted. Add the onion and cook, stirring occasionally, until tender and golden, about 20 minutes. Stir in the garlic, 1 teaspoon salt, cumin, coriander, allspice, and ¼ teaspoon pepper; cook for 1 minute.

3 Add the tomatoes and garbanzo beans to the skillet; heat to boiling over medium-high heat. Reduce heat to medium-low; simmer, stirring occasionally, 5 minutes.

4 Drain the pasta and return it to the saucepot. Toss the garbanzo bean mixture with the pasta; heat through. Toss with chopped parsley just before serving. Garnish with parsley sprigs.

EACH SERVING: ABOUT 400 CALORIES, 14G PROTEIN, 73G CARBOHYDRATE, 7G TOTAL FAT (2G SATURATED), 5G FIBER, 1,039MG SODIUM

Three-Bean Sweet Potato Chili
(page 81)

5 | Soups

What's better than a bowl of soup? A comforting broth with a bounty of fresh vegetables will always hit the spot. This chapter is chock-full of hearty soups sure to satisfy. We consider an occasional dose of comfort food an essential part of every diet. Besides, soup is a terrific vehicle for filling grains, noodles, and beans. Consider our wholesome Barley Minestrone, or add cooked grains like quinoa to your own creation. Three-Bean Sweet Potato Chili packs a whole lot of protein into a single bowl. Favorites like Red Lentil & Vegetable Soup and Vegan Black Bean Soup are also fabulous options. And soup is not limited to just fall and winter. Chilled soups like Gazpacho with Cilantro Cream are a great way to incorporate fresh vegetables into your summer diet. We offer many recipes to savor, so ladle up!

BARLEY
Minestrone

A bowlful of minestrone is always soothing.
Top it with a dollop of our quick and easy Homemade Vegan Pesto.

ACTIVE TIME: 50 MINUTES   **TOTAL TIME:** 1 HOUR 15 MINUTES   **MAKES:** 6 SERVINGS

1   cup pearl barley

olive oil

2   cups thinly sliced green cabbage
     (about ¼ small head)

2   large carrots, peeled, each cut lengthwise
     in half, then crosswise into ½-inch-thick
     slices

2   large stalks celery, cut into ½-inch dice

1   medium onion, cut into ½-inch dice

1   garlic clove, finely chopped

2   (14½-ounce) cans vegetable broth

1   (14½-ounce) can diced tomatoes

salt

1   medium zucchini (8 to 10 ounces),
     cut into ½-inch dice

4   ounces green beans, trimmed and cut
     into ½-inch pieces (1 cup)

Homemade Vegan Pesto

1 Heat a 5- to 6-quart Dutch oven over medium-high heat until hot. Add the barley and cook until toasted and fragrant, about 3 to 4 minutes, stirring constantly. Transfer the barley to a small bowl; set aside.

2 In the same Dutch oven, heat 1 tablespoon oil over medium-high heat until hot. Add the cabbage, carrots, celery, and onion; cook until the vegetables are tender and lightly browned, 8 to 10 minutes, stirring occasionally. Add the garlic and

cook until fragrant, 30 seconds. Stir in the barley, 3 cups water, broth, tomatoes with their juice, and ¼ teaspoon salt. Cover and heat to boiling over high heat. Reduce heat to low and simmer for 25 minutes.

3 Stir the zucchini and green beans into the barley mixture; increase heat to medium, cover, and cook until all the vegetables are barely tender, 10 to 15 minutes longer.

4 Meanwhile, prepare Homemade Vegan Pesto (below).

5 Ladle the minestrone into 6 large soup bowls. Top each serving with a dollop of pesto.

EACH SERVING: ABOUT 215 CALORIES, 7G PROTEIN, 42G CARBOHYDRATE, 4G TOTAL FAT (0G SATURATED), 9G FIBER, 690MG SODIUM

Homemade Vegan Pesto

Pulse **3 cups basil leaves**, **⅓ cup extra-virgin olive oil**, **¼ cup whole blanched almonds**, toasted (see page 51), and **2 small garlic cloves** in a food processor until very finely chopped. Sprinkle in salt and pepper and pulse to combine. Add a tablespoon or two of nutritional yeast, if you like.

EACH SERVING: ABOUT 135 CALORIES, 1G PROTEIN, 2G CARBOHYDRATE, 15G TOTAL FAT (2G SATURATED), 1G FIBER, 48MG SODIUM

Red Lentil &
VEGETABLE SOUP

This meal-in-a-bowl is brimming with fill-you-up soluble fiber, thanks to the lentils. Translation: It may help keep weight down and also helps lower total and "bad" LDL cholesterol.

ACTIVE TIME: 20 MINUTES   **TOTAL TIME:** 30 MINUTES   **MAKES:** 4 SERVINGS

olive oil

4   medium carrots, peeled and chopped

1   small onion, chopped

1   teaspoon ground cumin

1   (14½-ounce) can diced tomatoes

1   cup red lentils, rinsed and picked through

1   (14½-ounce) can vegetable broth

salt

ground black pepper

1   (5-ounce) package baby spinach

1 In a 4-quart saucepan, heat 1 tablespoon oil over medium heat until hot. Add the carrots and onion; cook until tender and lightly browned, 6 to 8 minutes. Stir in the cumin and cook for 1 minute.

2 Add the tomatoes with their juice, lentils, broth, 2 cups water, ¼ teaspoon salt, and ⅛ teaspoon pepper; cover and heat to boiling over high heat. Reduce heat to low; cover and simmer until the lentils are tender, 8 to 10 minutes.

3 Just before serving, stir in the spinach.

EACH SERVING: ABOUT 265 CALORIES, 16G PROTEIN, 41G CARBOHYDRATE, 5G TOTAL FAT (1G SATURATED), 13G FIBER, 645MG SODIUM

Tomato-Quinoa
SOUP

Protein-packed quinoa is the perfect addition
to this fresh, brightly flavored soup.

ACTIVE TIME: 15 MINUTES   **TOTAL TIME:** ABOUT 15 MINUTES   **MAKES:** 6 SERVINGS

1   cup red or white quinoa, rinsed

3   tablespoons vegan margarine or butter

olive oil

2   medium shallots, chopped

2   garlic cloves, chopped

1   tablespoon fennel seeds

2   (28-ounce) cans whole peeled tomatoes

2   cups low-sodium vegetable broth

2   cups roasted salted pepitas (pumpkin seeds)

1   tablespoon snipped fresh chives

1   teaspoon crushed red pepper

1 Cook the quinoa as the package label directs.

2 In a 4-quart saucepan, heat the margarine
and 1 tablespoon oil over medium heat until the
margarine melts. Add the shallots, garlic, and
fennel seeds. Cook for 4 to 6 minutes or until the
vegetables begin to soften, stirring occasionally.
Add the tomatoes and broth. Heat to simmering
on high. Simmer for 15 minutes, stirring
occasionally. With an immersion or regular
blender, puree the mixture until smooth. Reheat
the soup if necessary.

3 In a medium bowl, combine the cooked quinoa,
pepitas, chives, and crushed red pepper. Serve the
soup topped with the quinoa mixture.

EACH SERVING: ABOUT 275 CALORIES, 9G PROTEIN,
34G CARBOHYDRATE, 13G TOTAL FAT (5G SATURATED),
7G FIBER, 875MG SODIUM

Gazpacho
WITH CILANTRO CREAM

Recipes for gazpacho abound. This version is topped with a dollop of cilantro-spiked, nondairy sour cream—a tasty combination.

ACTIVE TIME: 30 MINUTES **TOTAL TIME:** 30 MINUTES, PLUS CHILLING **MAKES:** 4 CUPS

GAZPACHO

2   medium cucumbers (8 ounces each), peeled

1   medium yellow pepper (4 to 6 ounces)

¼   small red onion

2   pounds ripe tomatoes (5 medium), peeled, seeded, and chopped

½   to 1 small jalapeño chile, seeded

3   tablespoons fresh lime juice

extra-virgin olive oil

salt

CILANTRO CREAM

¼   cup nondairy sour cream or nondairy plain yogurt

1   tablespoon plain soy milk

4   teaspoons chopped fresh cilantro

salt

1 Prepare the Gazpacho: Coarsely chop half of 1 cucumber, half the yellow pepper, and all the onion; set aside. Cut remaining cucumbers and yellow pepper into large pieces for pureeing.

2 In a blender or food processor with the knife blade attached, puree large pieces of cucumber and yellow pepper, tomatoes, jalapeño, lime juice, 2 tablespoons oil, and ¾ teaspoon salt until smooth. Pour the puree into a bowl; add coarsely chopped cucumber, yellow pepper, and onion. Cover and refrigerate until well chilled, for at least 6 hours and up to overnight.

3 Prepare the Cilantro Cream: In a small bowl, stir the nondairy sour cream, soy milk, cilantro, and 1 teaspoon salt until smooth. Cover and refrigerate.

4 To serve, top soup with dollops of cilantro cream.

EACH SERVING: ABOUT 145 CALORIES, 3G PROTEIN, 15G CARBOHYDRATE, 9G TOTAL FAT (1G SATURATED), 4G FIBER, 539MG SODIUM

MOROCCAN-SPICED
Sweet Potato Medley

This fragrant stew is both heart-healthy and satisfying.

ACTIVE TIME: 15 MINUTES   **TOTAL TIME:** 45 MINUTES   **MAKES:** 4 SERVINGS

olive oil

1   medium yellow onion, chopped

3   garlic cloves, crushed

1½ teaspoons curry powder

1½ teaspoons ground cumin

¼   teaspoon ground allspice

1   (15-ounce) can diced tomatoes

1   (15-ounce) can low-sodium vegetable broth

1   cup no-salt-added garbanzo beans, drained and rinsed

1   large sweet potato (1 pound), peeled and cut into ¾-inch pieces

2   small zucchini (6 ounces each), cut into ¾-inch pieces

1   cup whole-grain couscous

¼   cup loosely packed fresh mint leaves, chopped

1 In a nonstick 12-inch skillet, heat 2 tablespoons oil over medium heat until hot. Add the onion and cook until tender and lightly browned, 8 to 10 minutes, stirring occasionally. Stir in the garlic, curry powder, cumin, and allspice; cook for 30 seconds.

2 Add the tomatoes, broth, beans, and sweet potato; cover and heat to boiling over medium-high heat. Reduce heat to medium and cook for 10 minutes.

3 Stir in the zucchini; cover and cook until the vegetables are tender, about 10 minutes.

4 Meanwhile, prepare the couscous as the package label directs.

5 Stir mint into the stew. Serve with couscous.

EACH SERVING: ABOUT 360 CALORIES, 14G PROTEIN, 70G CARBOHYDRATE, 5G TOTAL FAT (1G SATURATED), 13G FIBER, 670MG SODIUM

SPICED
Pumpkin Soup

This delicious soup delivers a double dose of antioxidants
with the combination of pumpkin and carrots.

ACTIVE TIME: 20 MINUTES   TOTAL TIME: 45 MINUTES   MAKES: 8 SERVINGS

12 tablespoons vegan stick margarine

1   medium carrot, peeled and
    finely chopped

1   medium onion, finely chopped

2   garlic cloves, minced

2   teaspoons ground cumin

½   teaspoon ground cinnamon

1   (32-ounce) carton vegetable broth

1   (29-ounce) can solid pack pumpkin

1   (12-ounce) can carrot juice

½   cup hulled pumpkin seeds (pepitas),
    roasted, for serving

1 In a 4-quart saucepan, melt the margarine over medium heat. Add carrot and onion; cook until soft, for about 8 to 10 minutes, stirring frequently. Add the garlic, cumin, and cinnamon; cook for 1 minute, stirring. Add the broth, pumpkin, and carrot juice to the saucepan, stirring to combine. Cover and heat to boiling over high heat. Reduce heat to low; cover and simmer for 15 minutes to blend flavors.

2 Stir soup just before serving. Pass pumpkin seeds around the table to sprinkle over soup.

EACH SERVING: ABOUT 190 CALORIES, 8G PROTEIN,
19G CARBOHYDRATE, 10G FAT (2G SATURATED),
5G FIBER, 570MG SODIUM

TIP

Make sure to look for pumpkin puree rather than pumpkin-pie mix in the grocery store.

Three-Bean
SWEET POTATO CHILI

This stick-to-your-ribs dish proves that vegetarian fare
can be just as filling as meaty meals. For photo, see page 72.

ACTIVE TIME: 20 MINUTES   **TOTAL TIME:** 1 HOUR   **MAKES:** 6 SERVINGS

1¼ pounds sweet potatoes

vegetable oil

1   medium onion

2   chipotle chiles in adobo

3   garlic cloves

1   tablespoon ground cumin

2   teaspoons chili powder

salt

2   (14½-ounce) cans diced tomatoes

1   (28-ounce) can puréed tomatoes

2   cups frozen shelled edamame

1   (15-ounce) can no-salt-added pinto beans

1   (15-ounce) can no-salt-added black beans

1 In a microwave-safe glass baking dish, combine sweet potatoes and 2 tablespoons water. Cover with vented plastic wrap and microwave on high for 12 minutes or until tender.

2 Meanwhile, in a 5-quart saucepot, heat 2 tablespoons oil over medium. Add the onion, chipotles, garlic, cumin, chili powder, and ¼ teaspoon salt. Cook for 5 minutes, stirring occasionally. Add tomatoes and 2 cups water. Heat on high to simmer; simmer for 15 minutes, stirring occasionally.

3 Add the sweet potatoes to the pot, along with the edamame, pinto beans, black beans, and ¼ teaspoon salt. Cook for 2 to 5 minutes or until beans are hot.

EACH SERVING: ABOUT 340 CALORIES, 16G PROTEIN, 54G CARBOHYDRATE, 7G TOTAL FAT (1G SATURATED), 16G FIBER, 750MG SODIUM

VEGAN
Black Bean Soup

Vegetables are the true star of this hearty, healthy soup, making it a perfect option for your vegan friends.

ACTIVE TIME: 20 MINUTES   **TOTAL TIME:** 4 HOURS, 50 MINUTES   **MAKES:** 6 SERVINGS

olive oil

2   medium carrots, chopped

2   stalks celery, sliced

1   medium onion, finely chopped

¼   cup tomato paste

3   garlic cloves, crushed

1½   teaspoons ground cumin

3   cups low-sodium vegetable broth

3   (15-ounce) cans low-sodium black beans, undrained

1   cup frozen corn

avocado chunks and cilantro leaves, for serving

1 In a 12-inch skillet, heat 2 tablespoons oil on medium-high. Add the carrots, celery, and onion. Cook for 6 to 8 minutes or until starting to brown, stirring occasionally. Add the tomato paste, garlic, and cumin. Cook, stirring, for 1 to 2 minutes or until garlic is golden and tomato paste has browned. Stir in ½ cup broth, scraping up any browned bits.

2 Transfer the contents of the skillet into a 6- to 8-quart slow-cooker bowl, along with the beans, corn, and remaining broth. Cover and cook on high for 4 hours or low for 6 hours. Serve with avocado and cilantro.

EACH SERVING: ABOUT 325 CALORIES, 14G PROTEIN, 51G CARBOHYDRATE, 11G TOTAL FAT (1G SATURATED), 19G FIBER, 535MG SODIUM

Roasted Butternut Squash with Pumpkin Seeds & Mole Sauce (page 90)

6 | Main Meals

So often we cook with what is in season, and these recipes feature vegetables available throughout the year. Stuffed Portobellos are great in the winter when accompanied by a side of roasted Brussels sprouts, another chilly-month staple. Bulgur & Cashew-Stuffed Eggplant and Coconut-Cauliflower Curry Bowls are delicious preparations in the summertime. And when the warm weather kicks up in the spring, brush off the grill for Grilled Asparagus & Shiitake Mushroom Tacos. If it's still too chilly, a grill pan on the stovetop works well, too. And, don't forget the tofu! A wonderful source of protein and iron, tofu is a flavor sponge. It soaks up wonderful sauces—check out our Hoisin-Ginger Tofu & Veggies—and is a delicious addition to any veggie-forward meal.

STUFFED
Portobellos

This healthy meal is low in calories, yet hearty enough to serve as a main course. Quinoa, which has a mild, slightly nutty flavor, packs more protein than any other grain.

ACTIVE TIME: 15 MINUTES   **TOTAL TIME:** 30 MINUTES   **MAKES:** 4 SERVINGS

½ cup quinoa

1¼ pounds Brussels sprouts

extra-virgin olive oil

salt

ground black pepper

4 large portobello mushroom caps

1 teaspoon fresh thyme leaves

⅔ cup frozen corn

3 ounces almond feta cheese

½ teaspoon ground cumin

1 Preheat your oven to 450°F. In a 2-quart saucepan, combine the quinoa and ¾ cup water. Heat to boiling; reduce heat to medium-low. Cover and cook for 15 minutes or until liquid is absorbed.

2 Meanwhile, trim and halve the Brussels sprouts. In an 18 x 12-inch jelly-roll pan, toss Brussels sprouts, 2 teaspoons oil, and ¼ teaspoon each salt and pepper to evenly coat. Roast for 10 minutes.

3 While the Brussels sprouts cook, brush the mushrooms with 2 teaspoons oil and sprinkle with ⅛ teaspoon salt. Finely chop the thyme and add to a medium bowl along with corn, feta, cumin, and cooked quinoa.

4 When the Brussels sprouts have roasted for 10 minutes, push them to one side of the pan and arrange the mushrooms, gill side up, on the other side. Divide the quinoa mixture among the mushrooms; roast for 10 minutes or until the mushrooms are tender.

EACH SERVING: ABOUT 290 CALORIES, 14G PROTEIN, 38G CARBOHYDRATE, 11G TOTAL FAT (4G SATURATED), 9G FIBER, 500MG SODIUM

TIP
Brussels sprouts not a favorite? Roasted broccoli delivers just as much crunch.

Bulgur &
CASHEW-STUFFED EGGPLANT

There's no meat or dairy but plenty of flavor in this heart-healthy meal. For photo, see page 11.

ACTIVE TIME: 10 MINUTES   TOTAL TIME: 30 MINUTES   MAKES: 4 SERVINGS

olive oil

3   garlic cloves, crushed

½   cup golden raisins

½   teaspoon curry powder

salt

1   cup quick-cooking bulgur

2   medium eggplants

½   cup cashews

chopped mint, for garnish

1 In a small saucepot, heat 1 tablespoon oil on medium. Add the garlic, golden raisins, curry powder, and ¼ teaspoon salt. Cook for 2 minutes, stirring. Add the bulgur and 2 cups water. Heat to a simmer and cover; simmer for 15 minutes or until bulgur is tender.

2 Meanwhile, cut the eggplants in half lengthwise. Scoop out the seeds. Arrange the eggplant on a foil-lined baking sheet, cut sides up. Brush with 2 tablespoons oil and sprinkle with ½ teaspoon salt. Broil on high (6 inches from the heat source) for 7 minutes or until tender.

3 Remove the eggplant from the oven; cover with foil. With a fork, fluff the bulgur; stir in the cashews. Stuff the eggplant with the bulgur mixture; garnish with chopped mint.

EACH SERVING: ABOUT 460 CALORIES, 11G PROTEIN, 69G CARBOHYDRATE, 19G TOTAL FAT (3G SATURATED), 16G FIBER, 450MG SODIUM

Stuffed Vegetables

If you've been preparing vegan meals, you've probably steamed, sautéed, stir-fried, and roasted vegetables. But have you tried stuffing them? We offer recipes for filling acorn squash, eggplant, and bell peppers, but you can stuff all sorts of vegetables to the brim with other vegetables, whole grains, or some delectable combination. Portobello mushrooms, zucchini halves, and tomatoes are all good candidates. Just scoop out the innards, brush with olive oil, fill, and roast in a 375°F oven until the veggies have softened and the filling has browned.

STUFFED
Acorn Squash

Pine nuts and cannellini beans impart rich flavor and texture to this wild rice–stuffed acorn squash. The squash halves create natural bowls, so just grab a spoon and dig in.

ACTIVE TIME: 35 MINUTES   TOTAL TIME: 55 MINUTES   MAKES: 4 SERVINGS

2   acorn squash (1½ pounds each), cut in half and seeded

olive oil

2   ounces vegan bacon, finely chopped (optional)

1   small onion (4 to 6 ounces), finely chopped

2   large stalks celery, finely chopped

⅛   teaspoon crushed red pepper flakes

salt

ground black pepper flakes

1   (15-ounce) can low-sodium cannellini beans, drained and rinsed

1   (7.4-ounce) package heat-and-serve precooked wild rice (do not heat)

4   teaspoons pine nuts (pignoli)

½   cup packed fresh basil leaves, thinly sliced, for garnish

1   Preheat your oven to 375°F. Line a 15½ x 10½-inch jelly-roll pan with foil. On a large microwave-safe plate, arrange the squash halves in a single layer, cut sides down. Microwave on High for 9 to 11 minutes or until a knife pierces the flesh easily.

2   Meanwhile, in a 12-inch skillet, heat 1 teaspoon oil over medium-high heat until hot. Add the vegan bacon pieces, if using, and cook for 3 to 4 minutes or until browned and crisp, stirring frequently. With a spatula, transfer to paper towels to drain. Add the onion, celery, crushed red pepper flakes, and ¼ teaspoon each salt and pepper to the skillet. Cook for 4 to 5 minutes or until the vegetables are tender and golden brown, stirring frequently. Remove from the heat. In a small bowl, mash ¼ cup beans with ¼ cup water. Into the vegetables in the skillet, stir the rice, mashed beans, whole beans, vegan bacon, 2 teaspoons pine nuts, and half of the basil. Season with salt and pepper to taste.

3   On a prepared jelly-roll pan, arrange the squash halves in a single layer, cut side up. Divide the bean mixture among the squash cavities, pressing firmly into the cavities and mounding on top. Cover the pan with foil. Bake for 15 minutes. Uncover and bake for 5 to 7 minutes longer or until squash and vegetables are golden on top. Garnish with the remaining pine nuts and basil.

EACH SERVING: ABOUT 320 CALORIES, 12G PROTEIN, 63G CARBOHYDRATE, 4G TOTAL FAT (0G SATURATED), 11G FIBER, 346MG SODIUM

Roasted Butternut Squash
WITH PUMPKIN SEEDS & MOLE SAUCE

This vegetarian squash bowl is so hearty and luscious,
you'll hardly miss the meat. For photo, see page 84.

ACTIVE TIME: 10 MINUTES   **TOTAL TIME:** 50 MINUTES   **MAKES:** 4 SERVINGS

1   large butternut squash, peeled
and cut into 1 inch chunks

olive oil

salt

ground black pepper

½   cup raw shelled pumpkin seeds,
plus more for garnish

½   teaspoon cumin seeds

½   teaspoon dried oregano

½   onion, cut into wedges

2   tomatillos, husked and halved

2   cloves garlic, halved

1   jalapeño chile, sliced

¾   cup vegetable stock

½   cup coconut milk

½   cup parsley, chopped

¼   cup packed cilantro, chopped,
plus more for garnish

lime wedges, for garnish

cooked rice, for serving

1 Preheat oven to 400°F. Toss squash with
2 tablespoons olive oil, 1 teaspoon salt, and
¼ teaspoon pepper. Arrange on baking sheet;
roast 35 to 40 minutes or until squash is tender,
stirring occasionally.

2 Meanwhile, in 10-inch skillet, toast pumpkin
seeds, cumin seeds, and oregano on medium
heat for 3 minutes or until fragrant, stirring.
Remove from heat; set aside. In same skillet, heat
1 tablespoon olive oil on medium. Add onion,
tomatillos, garlic, and jalapeño; cook 5 minutes
or until slightly browned. Place vegetables
and pumpkin-seed mixture in blender or food
processor. Pulse a few times; then add stock,
coconut milk, parsley, cilantro, ¾ teaspoon salt,
and ¼ teaspoon pepper. Process until smooth.
Makes 3 cups.

3 Return mixture to skillet; simmer on medium
heat, stirring often, for 15 to 20 minutes or until
slightly thickened. Divide rice and squash among
4 bowls; dollop with sauce. Serve remaining
sauce on the side. Garnish with cilantro and lime
wedges.

EACH SERVING: ABOUT 440 CALORIES, 10G PROTEIN,
60G CARBOHYDRATE, 19G TOTAL FAT (6G SATURATED),
5G FIBER, 605MG SODIUM

Japanese Eggplant &
TOFU STIR-FRY

Japanese eggplant is long and slender. When cooked,
it absorbs the wonderful flavor of the stir-fry sauce.
Serve with brown rice to get every drop.

ACTIVE TIME: 30 MINUTES   **TOTAL TIME:** 45 MINUTES, PLUS STANDING   **MAKES:** 4 SERVINGS

1 (16-ounce) package firm tofu, drained

1 cup vegetable broth

¼ cup low-sodium soy sauce

2 tablespoons brown sugar

2 tablespoons cornstarch

vegetable oil

4 medium Japanese eggplants (4 ounces each), cut diagonally into 2-inch pieces

8 ounces shiitake mushrooms, stems removed and caps cut into quarters

1 tablespoon grated, peeled fresh ginger

3 garlic cloves, crushed

3 green onions, thinly sliced

2 heads baby bok choy (6 ounces each), cut crosswise into 1-inch-thick slices

1 In a medium bowl, place four layers of paper towels; add the tofu and cover with four more layers of paper towels, pressing lightly to extract the liquid from the tofu. Let tofu stand for 10 minutes to drain, then cut into 1-inch cubes.

2 Meanwhile, in a 2-cup liquid measuring cup, with a fork or a wire whisk, combine ½ cup water, broth, soy sauce, brown sugar, and cornstarch, stirring until the brown sugar and cornstarch are dissolved; set aside.

3 In a deep 12-inch skillet or wok, heat 1 tablespoon oil over medium-high heat until hot. Add the eggplant and ⅓ cup water; cover and cook until the eggplant is tender, 7 to 10 minutes, stirring occasionally. Transfer the eggplant to a small bowl; set aside.

4 Add 1 tablespoon oil to the skillet and heat until hot. Add the mushrooms and tofu; cook until the tofu is lightly browned, about 5 minutes. Stir in the ginger, garlic, and half the green onions; cook for 1 minute, stirring. Add the bok choy and cook until the vegetables are lightly browned, about 4 minutes longer.

5 Stir the broth mixture; add to the tofu mixture with the eggplant. Heat to boiling over medium-high heat; reduce heat to low and simmer 1 minute, stirring. Sprinkle with remaining green onions before serving.

EACH SERVING: ABOUT 280 CALORIES, 15G PROTEIN, 33G CARBOHYDRATE, 13G TOTAL FAT (1G SATURATED), 5G FIBER, 865MG SODIUM

Coconut-Cauliflower
CURRY BOWLS

In the mood for some curry but don't want to order takeout?
This cauliflower-and-butternut squash version is ready in no time.

ACTIVE TIME: 10 MINUTES   **TOTAL TIME:** 40 MINUTES   **MAKES:** 6 SERVINGS

vegetable oil

2   medium shallots, chopped

2   tablespoons finely chopped, peeled fresh ginger

1   tablespoon curry powder

1   (20-ounce) package precut butternut squash chunks

1   (15-ounce) can coconut milk, shaken

1   (15-ounce) can fire-roasted diced tomatoes, drained

salt

4   cups cauliflower florets (about 12 ounces)

6   cups cooked white rice, for serving

cilantro leaves, for garnish

1 In a 6- to 7-quart saucepot, heat 1 tablespoon oil on medium. Add the shallots, ginger, and curry powder; cook for 5 minutes, stirring.

2 Add the squash, coconut milk, tomatoes, and 1 teaspoon salt. Cover and simmer 15 minutes. Uncover; stir in the cauliflower. Cook another 15 minutes or until the squash and cauliflower are tender, stirring occasionally.

3 Serve over rice. Garnish with cilantro.

EACH SERVING: ABOUT 445 CALORIES, 9G PROTEIN, 65G CARBOHYDRATE, 18G TOTAL FAT (14G SATURAED), 5G FIBER, 465MG SODIUM

TIP

Make-ahead: Proceed with recipe through adding cauliflower in step 2. After adding cauliflower, remove from heat, let cool, and refrigerate, covered, for up to 1 day (or hold at room temperature for up to 3 hours). Reheat on medium 25 to 30 minutes or until squash and cauliflower are tender. Continue with step 3.

BBQ Tempeh &
VEGETABLE KEBABS

Tempeh, or fermented cooked soybeans, is a great source of plant-based protein. It has a firm and chewy texture with an earthy yet sweet taste.

ACTIVE TIME: 30 MINUTES   **TOTAL TIME:** 40 MINUTES   **MAKES:** 6 SERVINGS

1   (8-ounce) package tempeh

⅔   cup barbecue sauce

1   medium red pepper, seeded and cut into 1-inch pieces

1   small red onion, cut into 6 wedges, each wedge halved

1   medium zucchini, cut into ¼-inch-thick half moons

canola oil

salt

ground black pepper

1   teaspoon chili powder

1 Prepare an outdoor grill for direct grilling over medium heat.

2 Cut the tempeh into 24 cubes, about 1-inch each.

3 Heat a nonstick 10-inch skillet over medium heat. Add the tempeh and barbecue sauce and simmer until the sauce thickens and sticks to the tempeh, about 15 minutes, stirring occasionally. Remove from heat.

4 Meanwhile, cut the red pepper into 1-inch pieces. Cut the onion into 6 wedges, then cut each in half crosswise. Cut the zucchini in half lengthwise, then crosswise into ¼-inch slices. In a medium bowl, toss the vegetables with 1 tablespoon oil, salt and pepper to taste, and chili powder.

5 Assemble 12 wooden skewers using everything twice, except the onion (use that only once).

6 Place the kebabs on an oiled grill. Grill, turning occasionally, until browned and tender, 12 to 15 minutes. Remove to a large platter.

EACH SERVING: ABOUT 160 CALORIES, 9G PROTEIN, 208G CARBOHYDRATE, 6G TOTAL FAT (1G SATURATED), 4G FIBER, 354 MG SODIUM

Hoisin-Ginger
TOFU & VEGGIES

A great hoisin-ginger glaze flavors tofu, zucchini, and red pepper. Be sure to buy extra-firm tofu; other varieties will fall apart while grilling.

ACTIVE TIME: 30 MINUTES   **TOTAL TIME:** 30 MINUTES   **MAKES:** 4 SERVINGS

HOISIN-GINGER GLAZE

½   cup hoisin sauce

2   garlic cloves, crushed

vegetable oil

1   tablespoon low-sodium soy sauce

1   tablespoon grated, peeled fresh ginger

1   tablespoon seasoned rice vinegar

⅛   teaspoon cayenne pepper

TOFU AND VEGGIES

1   (16-ounce) package extra-firm tofu, drained

2   medium zucchini (8 to 10 ounces each), each cut lengthwise into quarters, then crosswise in half

1   large red pepper (8 to 10 ounces), cut into quarters

1   bunch green onions, whole

vegetable oil

1 Prepare an outdoor grill for direct grilling over medium heat.

2 **Prepare Hoisin-Ginger Glaze:** In a small bowl, with a fork, mix the hoisin sauce, garlic, 1 tablespoon oil, soy sauce, ginger, vinegar, and cayenne until blended.

3 **Prepare Tofu and Veggies:** Cut the tofu horizontally into 4 pieces, then cut each piece crosswise in half. Place the tofu on paper towels; pat dry with additional paper towels. Arrange the tofu on a large plate and brush both sides with half of the glaze. Spoon the remaining half of the glaze into a medium bowl; add the zucchini and red pepper. Gently toss the vegetables to coat them with the glaze. On another plate, rub the green onions with 1 teaspoon oil.

4 Place the tofu, zucchini, and red pepper on the hot grill rack over medium heat. Grill the tofu for about 6 minutes, gently turning once with a wide metal spatula. Transfer the tofu to a platter; keep warm. Continue cooking the vegetables, transferring them to the platter with the tofu as they are done, until tender and browned, about 5 minutes longer. Add the green onions to the grill rack during the last minute of cooking time; transfer to the platter when tender.

EACH SERVING: ABOUT 245 CALORIES, 15G PROTEIN, 22G CARBOHYDRATE, 11G TOTAL FAT (1G SATURATED), 5G FIBER, 615MG SODIUM

Grilled Asparagus &
SHIITAKE MUSHROOM TACOS

For a fresh spin on Mexican, try these stellar veggie tacos.

ACTIVE TIME: 15 MINUTES   TOTAL TIME: 20 MINUTES   MAKES: 4 SERVINGS

canola oil

4   garlic cloves, crushed

1   teaspoon ground chipotle chile

1   pound asparagus, trimmed

kosher salt

8   ounces shiitake mushrooms, stems
    discarded

1   bunch green onions, trimmed

8   corn tortillas, warmed, 1 cup homemade
    or Perfect Guacamole (page 104),
    lime wedges, cilantro sprigs, and hot
    sauce, for serving

1 Heat a grill on medium. In a large baking dish, combine 3 tablespoons oil, garlic, chipotle, and ½ teaspoon salt. Add the asparagus, shiitakes, and green onions, and toss to coat. Grill the asparagus until tender and lightly charred, 5 to 6 minutes, turning occasionally. Grill the shiitakes and green onions until lightly charred, 4 to 5 minutes, turning occasionally. Transfer the grilled vegetables to a cutting board. 2 Cut the asparagus and green onions into 2-inch segments. Slice the shiitakes. Serve with corn tortillas, guacamole, lime wedges, cilantro, and hot sauce.

EACH SERVING: ABOUT 350 CALORIES, 7G PROTEIN, 36G CARBOHYDRATE, 21G TOTAL FAT (2G SATURATED), 11G FIBER, 445MG SODIUM

Sweet Potato &
BLACK BEAN TACOS

Swap ground beef for spicy sweet potatoes
for the ultimate vegetarian taco.

ACTIVE TIME: 15 MINUTES **TOTAL TIME:** 40 MINUTES **MAKES:** 4 SERVINGS

1¼ pounds sweet potatoes, scrubbed and
cut into ½-inch chunks

olive oil

1 teaspoon chili powder

salt

1 (15-ounce) can no-salt-added black beans,
drained and rinsed

½ cup salsa verde

1 avocado, thinly sliced

8 corn tortillas

¼ cup crumbled vegan feta or cotija cheese

cilantro, for garnish

1 Toss the sweet potatoes with 1 tablespoon oil,
chili powder, and ½ teaspoon salt. Arrange on a
large rimmed baking sheet; roast for 30 minutes
in a 450°F oven.

2 In a saucepan, combine the black beans with
the salsa verde; cook on medium until warm,
stirring.

3 Serve the sweet potatoes and beans with
avocado, corn tortillas, cheese, and cilantro.

EACH SERVING: ABOUT 465 CALORIES, 13G PROTEIN,
70G CARBOHYDRATE, 16G TOTAL FAT (3G SAT), 16G
FIBER, 715MG SODIUM

Lemony Hummus
(page 106)

7 Snacks

One of the biggest challenges of the vegan diet can be finding nourishing snacks. This chapter delivers a roster of tasty snacks that you can reach for whenever you need a quick bite. It will take a little forethought and organization—you don't want to be whipping together hummus while completely ravenous—but we've provided lots of delicious recipes that you can prepare and keep on hand in the fridge, at work, or at home. If you're hankering for a savory snack, our Cracked-Wheat Pretzels or Hot-Pepper Nuts are easy to pack and pop in your mouth while you're on the go. We also provide a wide variety of dips—from guacamole to hummus to luscious Lemon-Cilantro-Eggplant Dip. Add some carrot or celery sticks and you have a quick and easy snack that's as good for you as it tastes.

Vegan Nacho Cheese &
CRISPY POTATOES

This vegan nacho sauce is so good,
it might even be better than cheese.

ACTIVE TIME: 15 MINUTES   **TOTAL TIME:** 45 MINUTES   **MAKES:** 4 SERVINGS

2	pounds mixed baby potatoes, halved
	canola oil
	salt
	ground black pepper
1	cup raw unsalted cashews, soaked overnight and drained
3	tablespoons lemon juice
½	teaspoon chili powder
½	teaspoon ground cumin
½	teaspoon sweet paprika
½	teaspoon garlic powder
1	teaspoon coarse sea salt
¼	cup nutritional yeast
½	jalapeño chile, seeded and chopped

1 Preheat your oven to 450°F. Toss the potatoes with 3 tablespoons oil, ½ teaspoon salt, and ¼ teaspoon pepper. On a rimmed baking sheet, spread the potatoes evenly; roast for 30 minutes until golden and crispy, stirring once.

2 Meanwhile, in a blender, puree the cashews, lemon juice, chili powder, cumin, paprika, garlic powder, sea salt, nutritional yeast, and jalapeño with 1 cup water until smooth. Transfer the mixture to a 2-quart saucepan; heat on medium-low for 5 minutes or until warm, stirring occasionally. Transfer to a bowl. Serve nacho cheese with the roasted potatoes.

EACH SERVING: ABOUT 380 CALORIES, 10G PROTEIN, 47G CARBOHYDRATE, 18G TOTAL FAT (2G SATURATED), 6G FIBER, 520MG SODIUM

TIP

Leftover sauce can be refrigerated for up to 1 day. The sauce is also good with tortilla chips, roasted cauliflower, or other roasted vegetables.

THE PERFECT
Guacamole

While guacamole is usually served as a dip, don't forget that it's a great accompaniment for tacos or burritos or on top of a veggie burger.

ACTIVE TIME: 15 MINUTES   **TOTAL TIME:** 15 MINUTES   **MAKES:** 1¾ CUPS

1   jalapeño chile, seeded and finely chopped

⅓   cup loosely packed fresh cilantro leaves, chopped

¼   cup finely chopped sweet onion, such as Vidalia or Maui

salt

2 ripe avocados

1 plum tomato

plain tortilla chips, for serving

1   In a mortar, combine jalapeño, cilantro, onion, and ½ teaspoon salt; with a pestle, grind until mixture becomes juicy and thick (onion can remain slightly chunky).

2   Cut each avocado lengthwise in half around the seed. Twist the halves in opposite directions to separate. Slip a spoon between the seed and the fruit, and work the seed out. With a spoon, scoop the fruit from the peel and onto a cutting board.

3 Cut the tomato crosswise in half. Squeeze the halves to remove the seeds and juice. Coarsely chop the tomato.

4 If the mortar is large enough, add the avocado and chopped tomato to the onion mixture in the mortar. (If the mortar is too small, combine the avocado, tomato, and onion mixture in a bowl.) Mash slightly with a pestle or spoon until the mixture is blended but still somewhat chunky.

5 Guacamole is best when served as soon as it's made. If you're not serving it right away, press plastic wrap directly onto the surface of the guacamole to prevent discoloration and refrigerate for up to 1 hour. Serve with chips.

EACH SERVING (1 TABLESPOON): ABOUT 25 CALORIES, 0G PROTEIN, 1G CARBOHYDRATE, 2G TOTAL FAT (0G SATURATED), 3G FIBER, 45MG SODIUM

 TIP

Our favorite avocados for guacamole are the varieties with thick, pebbly, green skin, such as Hass, Pinkerton, and Reed.

ROASTED
Red Pepper Dip

A tasty dip with a Middle Eastern accent.
Serve with vegetables and pita chips, or spread it on a sandwich.

ACTIVE TIME: 45 MINUTES   TOTAL TIME: 45 MINUTES   MAKES: 2 CUPS

4   red peppers, roasted (see below)

½   teaspoon ground cumin

½   cup walnuts, toasted

2   slices firm white bread, torn into pieces

2   tablespoons vinegar, preferably raspberry

olive oil

salt

⅛   teaspoon cayenne pepper

toasted pita bread wedges, for serving

1 Cut the roasted peppers into large pieces. In a small skillet, toast the cumin over low heat, stirring constantly, until very fragrant, 1 to 2 minutes.

2 In a food processor with the knife blade attached, process the walnuts until ground. Add the roasted peppers, cumin, bread, vinegar, 1 tablespoon oil, ½ teaspoon salt, and cayenne; puree until smooth. Transfer to a bowl. If you're not serving right away, cover and refrigerate for up to 4 hours. Serve with toasted pita bread wedges.

EACH SERVING (1 TABLESPOON): ABOUT 23 CALORIES, 0G PROTEIN, 2G CARBOHYDRATE, 2G TOTAL FAT (0G SATURATED), 0G FIBER, 46MG SODIUM

Roasted
Red Peppers

Preheat your oven's broiler. Line a broiling pan with foil. Cut the **4 red peppers** lengthwise in half; remove and discard the stems and seeds. Arrange the peppers, cut side down, in the prepared broiling pan. Place the pan under the broiler, 5 to 6 inches from the heat source. Broil, without turning, until the skin is charred and blistered, 8 to 10 minutes. Remove the peppers from heat, wrap in foil, and allow to steam at room temperature for 15 minutes or until cool enough to handle. Remove the peppers from the foil. Peel and discard the skin.

LEMONY
Hummus

You can buy hummus readymade at the grocery store,
but making your own is so much more satisfying
and economical. For photo, see page 100.

ACTIVE TIME: 15 MINUTES   **TOTAL TIME:** 15 MINUTES, PLUS CHILLING   **MAKES:** 2 CUPS

4 garlic cloves, peeled

1 large lemon

1 (15- to 19-ounce) can garbanzo beans,
drained and rinsed

2 tablespoons tahini (sesame seed paste)

olive oil

salt

⅛ teaspoon cayenne pepper

½ teaspoon paprika and 2 tablespoons
chopped fresh cilantro, for garnish

toasted pita bread wedges and olives, for
serving

1 In a 1-quart saucepan, heat 2 cups water to
boiling over high heat. Add the garlic and cook
for 3 minutes to blanch; drain.

2 From the lemon, grate 1 teaspoon peel and
squeeze 3 tablespoons juice. In a food processor
with the knife blade attached, combine the
beans, tahini, blanched garlic, lemon peel and
juice, 3 tablespoons oil, 2 tablespoons water,
½ teaspoon salt, and cayenne. Puree until
smooth. Transfer to a bowl; cover and refrigerate
for up to 4 hours.

3 To serve, sprinkle with paprika and cilantro.
Serve with pita bread wedges and olives.

EACH SERVING (1 TABLESPOON): ABOUT 28 CALORIES,
1G PROTEIN, 2G CARBOHYDRATE, 2G TOTAL FAT
(0G SATURATED), 3G FIBER, 54MG SODIUM

TIP

Tahini is readily available at health-food
stores and supermarkets.

LEMON-CILANTRO-
Eggplant Dip

The light, nutty flavor of tahini pairs perfectly
with rich roasted eggplant.

ACTIVE TIME: 10 MINUTES   **TOTAL TIME:** 55 MINUTES, PLUS CHILLING   **MAKES:** 2 CUPS

nonstick cooking spray

2   eggplants (1 pound each), each halved
    lengthwise

4   garlic cloves, unpeeled

3   tablespoons tahini (sesame seed paste)

3   tablespoons fresh lemon juice

salt

¼   cup loosely packed fresh cilantro or mint
    leaves, chopped

toasted or grilled pita bread wedges,
    carrot and cucumber sticks, and red or
    yellow pepper slices, for serving

1 Preheat your oven to 450°F. Line a 15½ x
10½-inch jelly-roll pan with foil and spray with
nonstick cooking spray. Place the eggplant halves,
skin sides up, in a foil-lined pan. Wrap the garlic
in foil and place in the pan with the eggplants.
Roast for 45 to 50 minutes or until the eggplants
are very tender and the skin is shriveled and
browned. Unwrap the garlic. Cool the eggplants
and garlic until they are easy to handle.

2 When cool, scoop the eggplant flesh into a food
processor with the knife blade attached. Squeeze
out the garlic pulp from each clove and add to the
food processor with the tahini, lemon juice, and
¾ teaspoon salt; pulse to coarsely chop. Spoon
the dip into a serving bowl; stir in the cilantro.
Cover and refrigerate for at least 2 hours. Serve
the dip with toasted pita bread wedges and
vegetables.

EACH SERVING (1 TABLESPOON): ABOUT 10 CALORIES,
0G PROTEIN, 2G CARBOHYDRATE, 0G TOTAL FAT
(0G SATURATED), 1G FIBER, 55MG SODIUM

SNACKS

CRACKED-WHEAT
Pretzels

This is a great way to receive a double shot
of whole-grain goodness at snack time.

ACTIVE TIME: 45 MINUTES   **TOTAL TIME:** 1 HOUR, PLUS STANDING   **MAKES:** 12 SERVINGS

¼   cup cracked wheat (coarse)

1½ cups all-purpose flour

1   package quick-rise yeast

2   teaspoons sugar

salt

1½ cups stone-ground whole wheat flour

1   tablespoon baking soda

1   teaspoon kosher salt

1 In a small bowl, pour 1 cup boiling water over
the cracked wheat. Cover the bowl with plastic
wrap and let stand for 30 minutes. Pour into a
large sieve and drain.

2 In a large bowl, combine the all-purpose flour,
1¼ cups very warm (120°F to 130°F) water, yeast,
sugar, and 1 teaspoon salt; stir to dissolve. Stir
in the whole wheat flour and drained cracked
wheat. Mix well with a wooden spoon. Knead
the dough until it's smooth and elastic, 4 to 6
minutes. Shape the dough into a ball; place in
a greased large bowl, turning the dough over to
grease the top. Cover the bowl and let rest for
10 minutes.

3 Preheat your oven to 400°F. Grease 2 large
cookie sheets. Punch down the dough and cut
it into 12 equal pieces. Roll each piece into a
20-inch-long rope. Shape the ropes into pretzels
and place 1½ inches apart on the prepared cookie
sheets. Let rise for 10 minutes.

4 In a small bowl, whisk ¼ cup very warm water
with the baking soda until soda dissolves. Brush
the baking soda mixture onto the pretzels and
sprinkle with kosher salt. Bake the pretzels,
rotating sheets between the upper and lower
racks halfway through baking, until browned,
16 to 18 minutes. Transfer to wire racks to cool.
Serve warm or at room temperature.

EACH SERVING: ABOUT 138 CALORIES, 5G PROTEIN,
28G CARBOHYDRATE, 1G TOTAL FAT (0G SATURATED),
3G FIBER, 670MG SODIUM

Kale CHIPS

Our crispy kale chips are virtually fat free—
perfect for guilt-free snacking.

ACTIVE TIME: 10 MINUTES   **TOTAL TIIME:** 12 MINUTES   **MAKES:** 6 SERVINGS

10   ounces kale, rinsed and dried well

nonstick cooking spray

kosher salt

Preheat your oven to 350°F. Remove and discard the thick stems from the kale, and tear the leaves into large pieces. Spread the leaves in a single layer on 2 large cookie sheets. Spray the leaves with nonstick cooking spray to coat lightly; sprinkle with ½ teaspoon salt. Bake for 12 to 15 minutes or just until crisp but not browned. Cool on the cookie sheets on wire racks.

EACH SERVING: ABOUT 15 CALORIES, 1G PROTEIN, 3G CARBOHYDRATE, 0G TOTAL FAT (0G SATURATED), 1G FIBER, 175MG SODIUM

PAPRIKA-PARMESAN
Granola Bars

Crumble these bars for a great salad garnish.

ACTIVE TIME: 10 MINUTES   **TOTAL TIME:** 40 MINUTES   **MAKES:** 8 BARS

1   cup rolled oats, toasted

½   cup crisp rice cereal

½   cup vegan Parmesan, grated

½   cup freeze-dried vegetable bits

⅓   cup smoked almonds, chopped

3   tablespoons chia seeds

½   teaspoon smoked paprika (swap in cumin, chili powder, or garlic powder for paprika)

kosher salt

ground black pepper

2   tablespoons flax seeds, ground

½   cup unsweetened nut butter

1 Line an 8 x 8-inch metal pan with foil; grease the foil. In a bowl, combine the rolled oats, crisp rice cereal, Parmesan, freeze-dried vegetable bits, smoked almonds, chia seeds, smoked paprika, and ½ teaspoon each salt and pepper. Stir together the flax seeds with 6 tablespoons water until combined. Add the flax seed mixture and unsweetened nut butter. Press firmly into the pan.
2 Bake at 350°F for 30 minutes. Cool completely on a wxire rack. Remove from the pan; cut into 8 bars. Store in an airtight container at room temperature for up to 1 week.

EACH SERVING: ABOUT 235 CALORIES, 10G PROTEIN, 18G CARBOHYDRATE, 1G TOTAL FAT (2G SATURATED), 5G FIBER, 300MG SODIUM

Choco-Cherry
BARS

These no-bake quinoa, oat, and chia treats make
a great grab-and-go breakfast or snack.

ACTIVE TIME: 15 MINUTES   TOTAL TIME: 1 HOUR AND 15 MINUTES   MAKES: 14 BARS

2   cups old-fashioned oats

½   cup quinoa

½   cup chia seeds

½   cup sliced almonds

½   cup dried cherries

½   cup chopped dark chocolate

¾   cup creamy almond butter

⅓   cup honey or agave nectar

coconut oil

salt

½   cup pureed prunes
     (from about 1 cup prunes)

1 Line a large baking sheet with parchment paper.

2 In a large bowl, combine the oats, quinoa, chia seeds, almonds, cherries, and chocolate.

3 In a small saucepan on low, heat the almond butter, honey or agave nectar, 2 tablespoons coconut oil, and ½ teaspoon salt until melted and smooth, stirring occasionally. Stir in the prune puree.

4 Pour the almond butter mixture over the oat mixture and stir to combine.

5 With your hands, form into bars, using about ⅓ cup mixture for each; place on the prepared baking sheet and refrigerate until set, about 1 hour. Store in the refrigerator in an airtight container for up to 3 weeks.

EACH SERVING: ABOUT 300 CALORIES, 7G PROTEIN, 35G CARBOHYDRATE, 17G TOTAL FAT (4G SATURATED), 6G FIBER, 105MG SODIUM

Hot-Pepper NUTS

You can use cashews, pecans, almonds, or any nuts you like!

ACTIVE TIME: 5 MINUTES   TOTAL TIME: 30 MINUTES   MAKES: 2 CUPS

nonstick cooking spray

2   cups (8 ounces) walnuts

1   tablespoon vegan stick margarine or
    butter, melted

2   teaspoons soy sauce

½   to 2 teaspoons hot pepper sauce

1 Preheat your oven to 350°F. Lightly grease
a jelly-roll pan with nonstick cooking spray.

2 In the prepared jelly-roll pan, toss the walnuts
with melted margarine until coated. Bake the
walnuts, stirring occasionally, until well toasted,
about 25 minutes. Drizzle the soy sauce and hot
pepper sauce over the nuts, tossing until well
mixed. Cool completely in the pan on a wire rack.
Store the nuts in an airtight container for up to
1 month.

EACH SERVING (¼ CUP): ABOUT 210 CALORIES,
4G PROTEIN, 6G CARBOHYDRATE, 21G TOTAL FAT
(3G SATURATED), 2G FIBER, 116MG SODIUM

Curried Nuts

Prepare the nuts as directed, but substitute
**1 teaspoon curry powder, ½ teaspoon ground
cumin**, and **½ teaspoon salt** for the soy sauce
and hot pepper sauce.

EACH SERVING (¼ CUP): ABOUT 216 CALORIES,
5G PROTEIN, 4G CARBOHYDRATE, 21G TOTAL FAT
(2G SATURATED), 2G FIBER, 185MG SODIUM

Chili Nuts

Prepare the nuts as directed above, but substitute
1 tablespoon chili powder and **½ teaspoon salt**
for the soy sauce and hot pepper sauce.

EACH SERVING (¼ CUP): ABOUT 215 CALORIES,
5G PROTEIN, 4G CARBOHYDRATE, 22G TOTAL FAT
(2G SATURATED), 2G FIBER, 185MG SODIUM

Sweet & Spicy Nuts

Prepare the nuts as directed, but substitute
**2 tablespoons sugar, 1½ teaspoons vegan
Worcestershire sauce, ½ teaspoon cayenne
pepper**, and **¼ teaspoon salt** for the soy sauce
and hot pepper sauce.

EACH SERVING (¼ CUP): ABOUT 230 CALORIES,
5G PROTEIN, 8G CARBOHYDRATE, 21G TOTAL FAT
(2G SATURATED), 2G FIBER, 185MG SODIUM

Orange Granita
(page 118)

8 Desserts

Living a vegan lifestyle does not mean you must skip the treats—if you plan accordingly and use baking substitutes, you can have healthy, vegan-friendly baked goods, too. So rest assured that these fabulous options will curb your sweet tooth when you have a craving. Bake some Deep-Chocolate Cupcakes or Oatmeal-Raisin Cookies and you'll be prepared when the urge hits. If you want to maintain a clean-food diet, fruit is a good snack to reach for when you yearn for something sweet. From various flavors of granitas for warmer months to delicious Stuffed Fresh Figs with Almond Ricotta, we have your options covered.

Orange GRANITA

Whip up this fancy Italian-style flavored ice
with only three ingredients. For photo, see page 116.

ACTIVE TIME: 45 MINUTES   TOTAL TIME: 1 HOUR, PLUS 5 HOURS FREEZING   MAKES: 6 SERVINGS

11   large navel oranges

½   cup sugar

salt

1 Cut the top quarter off 6 oranges; set aside. Trim the bottoms so they stand upright. With a small knife and spoon, scrape the pulp into a bowl; place the shells in the freezer. Into a 4-cup measuring cup, squeeze the juice from the pulp.

2 From 5 more oranges, grate 1 tablespoon peel and squeeze enough juice to make 3 cups in all. Stir in the sugar and a pinch of salt to dissolve; pour into a square metal baking pan.

3 Freeze for 5 hours, scraping the frozen bits with a fork every hour. To serve, scoop into the frozen shells and replace the tops.

EACH SERVING: 120 CALORIES, 1G PROTEIN, 30G CARBOHYDRATE, 0G TOTAL FAT (0G SATURATED), 0G FIBER, 21MG SODIUM

Very Berry GRANITA

We love using raspberries or blackberries
in this granita, but you can use blueberries or
a combination of berries, if you like.

ACTIVE TIME: 15 MINUTES **TOTAL TIME:** 20 MINUTES, PLUS COOLING AND FREEZING **MAKES:** 16 SERVINGS

1   cup sugar

6   cups raspberries or blackberries

2   tablespoons fresh lime juice

1 In a 2-quart saucepan, combine the sugar and 1¼ cups water; heat to boiling over high heat, stirring until the sugar has dissolved. Reduce the heat to medium and cook for 1 minute. Set the saucepan in a bowl of ice water until the syrup is cool.

2 Meanwhile, in a blender or in a food processor with the knife blade attached, puree the raspberries until smooth. With a spoon, press the puree through a sieve and into a medium bowl; discard the seeds.

3 Stir the sugar syrup and lime juice into the puree; pour into an 8-inch square metal baking pan. Cover and freeze until partially frozen, about 2 hours. Stir with a fork to break up chunks. Cover and freeze until completely frozen, for at least 3 hours or up to overnight. To serve, let stand at room temperature until slightly softened, about 15 minutes. Use a metal spoon to scrape across the surface of the granita, transferring ice shards to chilled dessert dishes or wine goblets without packing them.

EACH SERVING: ABOUT 70 CALORIES, 0G PROTEIN, 18G CARBOHYDRATE, 0G TOTAL FAT (0G SATURATED), 2G FIBER, 0MG SODIUM

Watermelon Granita

Prepare the syrup as directed in step 1, but use **¾ cup water**. Remove the rind and seeds from **1 piece (5½ pounds) watermelon**; cut fruit into bite-size pieces (9 cups). In a blender or in a food processor with the knife blade attached, in batches, puree watermelon until smooth. Press through a sieve into a large bowl; discard the fibers. Stir the **sugar syrup** and **lime juice** into the watermelon puree. Freeze as directed. Makes about 9 cups or 18 servings.

EACH SERVING: ABOUT 70 CALORIES, 0G PROTEIN, 17G CARBOHYDRATE, 0G TOTAL FAT (0G SATURATED), 0G FIBER, 2MG SODIUM

Stuffed FRESH FIGS

Figs are a good source of dietary fiber and potassium—
and did we mention that they're delicious?

ACTIVE TIME: 25 MINUTES TOTAL TIME: 25 MINUTES MAKES: 6 SERVINGS

19 small fresh ripe figs (1¼ pounds)

¼ cup maple syrup

½ cup Almond Ricotta

¼ cup natural almonds, toasted
   and chopped

1 On a plate, with a fork, mash the ripest fig with maple syrup; set aside.

2 With a sharp knife, trim the stems from the remaining figs, then cut a deep X in the top of each, making sure not to cut all the way through to the bottom. With your fingertips, gently spread each fig apart to make "petals."

3 In a small bowl, combine the Almond Ricotta and almonds. With the back of a spoon, press the mashed fig mixture through a sieve into a 1-cup measuring cup.

4 To serve, spoon the ricotta mixture into the figs. Arrange the figs on a platter. Drizzle with the fig maple syrup.

EACH SERVING: ABOUT 185 CALORIES, 3G PROTEIN, 30G CARBOHYDRATE, 7G TOTAL FAT (1G SATURATED), 4G FIBER, 52MG SODIUM

Almond Ricotta

Place ½ cup whole blanched almonds, 1½ cups warm water, 1 tablespoon lemon juice, ¼ teaspoon salt, and 1 tablespoon olive oil in a blender; blend until completely smooth, about 3 minutes. Pour the mixture into a medium saucepan. Heat to a simmer over medium heat; simmer until thickened, about 2 minutes, stirring frequently. Remove from heat and use as desired or cool and store in the refrigerator. Makes 1 cup.

EACH SERVING (1 CUP): ABOUT 545 CALORIES, 16G PROTEIN, 16G CARBOHYDRATE, 50G TOTAL FAT (5G SATURATED), 8G FIBER, 602MG SODIUM

TIP

The season for fresh figs is short and they're expensive, so if you indulge in them, be sure to get your money's worth. Buy fruit that is heavy, smells fresh (not musty), and is soft to the touch. Use them promptly; figs will keep, refrigerated, for only a day or two. Rinse figs gently before using them. The entire fruit is edible, skin and all. Just discard the stem.

Oatmeal-Raisin
COOKIES

Use vegan stick butter, not spread (which has a lower fat content),
or your cookie dough won't have the right consistency.

ACTIVE TIME: 35 MINUTES   TOTAL TIME: 1 HOUR   MAKES: 36 COOKIES

nonstick cooking spray

1   cup all-purpose flour

1   teaspoon ground cinnamon

½   teaspoon baking soda

½   teaspoon salt

¾   cup vegan stick butter or margarine

¾   cup packed brown sugar

⅓   cup granulated sugar

½   cup plain soy milk

1   teaspoon vanilla extract

3   cups old-fashioned oats

1   cup raisins

1   cup walnuts, chopped

1 Preheat your oven to 350°F. Spray 3 large baking sheets with nonstick cooking spray. In a small bowl, whisk the flour, cinnamon, baking soda, and salt.

2 In a large bowl, beat the butter, brown sugar, and granulated sugar until smooth and fluffy. Beat in soy milk and vanilla (it will look curdled; that's okay). Beat in the flour mixture. Stir in the oats, raisins, and walnuts.

3 Drop dough by heaping tablespoons onto the prepared baking sheets, 2 inches apart. Bake one sheet at a time until the cookies look dry and are browned at the edges, 13 to 15 minutes. Let them stand on the baking sheet for 1 minute before removing with a wide spatula to a wire rack to cool completely.

EACH COOKIE: ABOUT 135 CALORIES, 2G PROTEIN, 18G CARBOHYDRATE, 6G TOTAL FAT (2G SATURATED), 9G FIBER, 93MG SODIUM

Deep-Chocolate
CUPCAKES

Be sure to read the package labels since not all chocolates
are created equal, and some include milk solids.

ACTIVE TIME: 25 MINUTES   TOTAL TIME: 45 MINUTES   MAKES: 12 CUPCAKES

CUPCAKES

1½ cups all-purpose flour

¾   cup granulated sugar

⅛   cup unsweetened cocoa, sifted

¾   teaspoon baking soda

½   teaspoon salt

⅛   cup canola oil

1   tablespoon cider vinegar

1½ teaspoons vanilla extract

FROSTING

1½ cups confectioners' sugar

3   tablespoons vegan stick butter
    or margarine

1   to 2 tablespoons plain soy milk

½   teaspoon vanilla extract

3   ounces vegan bittersweet chocolate,
    melted and cooled

1 Prepare the Cupcakes: Preheat your oven
to 350°F. Line a 12-cup muffin pan with paper
liners.

2 In a large bowl, whisk the flour, granulated
sugar, cocoa, baking soda, and salt until blended.
Add 1 cup cold water, oil, cider vinegar, and
vanilla; whisk until the batter is smooth. Spoon
the batter evenly into the muffin cups. Bake until
a toothpick inserted into the center of a cupcake
comes out clean, 20 to 25 minutes. Remove the
cupcakes to a wire rack to cool completely.

3 Prepare the Frosting: While the cupcakes are
baking, in a medium bowl, beat the confectioners'
sugar, butter, 1 tablespoon soy milk, and vanilla
until smooth. Beat in the chocolate until the
frosting is light and fluffy, adding remaining
soy milk as needed to achieve easy spreading
consistency. Spread the frosting on the cooled
cupcakes. Top with dark chocolate shavings, if
desired.

EACH CUPCAKE: ABOUT 285 CALORIES, 3G PROTEIN,
45G CARBOHYDRATE, 12G TOTAL FAT (3G SATURATED),
2G FIBER, 208MG SODIUM

Index

Note: Page references in *italics* indicate photographs.

Photography Credits

FRONT and BACK COVER: Mike Garten

© Yossy Arefi : 38

Mike Garten: 2, 6, 9, 12, 14, 21, 30, 44, 49, 57, 58, 65, 67, 83, 84, 92, 97, 100, 103, 111, 112,

Getty images: © Eisenhut & Mayer 60, © Dave King Dorling Kindersley 22, © Rob Lawson 107 (eggplant), © Lew Robertson 52, © Lorenzo Vecchia 19, © Russ Witherington / EyeEm 51

iStockphoto: © Anna1311 43, © Ansonsaw 79, © Assalve 81 (chili), © Chengyuzheng 47, © Edim B 69, © Floortje 75, © Gaffera 63, © Hyrma 32, © MariusFM77 107, © Pzijl 109, © scisettialfio 81 (curry), © SrdicPhoto 118, © Viktorkunz 105

© Con Poulos: 26, 54, 87, 116

StockFood: © Amanda Stockley 115, © Brian Enright 123

Studio D: Chris Eckert 7

© Danielle Occhiogrosso: 46, 99

© Emily Kate Roemer: 11, 41

© Christopher Testani: 72, 77

Metric Conversion Charts

The recipes that appear in this cookbook use the standard United States method for measuring liquid and dry or solid ingredients (teaspoons, tablespoons, and cups). The information on this chart is provided to help cooks outside the U.S. successfully use these recipes. All equivalents are approximate.

METRIC EQUIVALENTS FOR DIFFERENT TYPES OF INGREDIENTS

STANDARD CUP (e.g., flour)	FINE POWDER (e.g., rice)	GRAIN (e.g., sugar)	GRANULAR (e.g., butter)	LIQUID SOLIDS (e.g., milk)	LIQUID
¾	105 g	113 g	143 g	150 g	180 ml
⅔	93 g	100 g	125 g	133 g	160 ml
½	70 g	75 g	95 g	100 g	120 ml
⅓	47 g	50 g	63 g	67 g	80 ml
¼	35 g	38 g	48 g	50 g	60 ml
⅛	18 g	19 g	24 g	25 g	30 ml

USEFUL EQUIVALENTS FOR LIQUID INGREDIENTS BY VOLUME

¼ tsp	=						1 ml
½ tsp	=						2 ml
1 tsp	=						5 ml
3 tsp	=	1 tbsp	=		½ fl oz	=	15 ml
		2 tbsp	=	⅛ cup	1 fl oz	=	30 ml
		4 tbsp	=	¼ cup	2 fl oz	=	60 ml
		5⅓ tbsp	=	⅓ cup	3 fl oz	=	80 ml
		8 tbsp	=	½ cup	4 fl oz	=	120 ml
		10⅔ tbsp	=	⅔ cup	5 fl oz	=	160 ml
		12 tbsp	=	¾ cup	6 fl oz	=	180 ml
		16 tbsp	=	1 cup	8 fl oz	=	240 ml
		1 pt	=	2 cups	16 fl oz	=	480 ml
		1 qt	=	4 cups	32 fl oz	=	960 ml
					33 fl oz	=	1000 ml = 1 L

USEFUL EQUIVALENTS FOR DRY INGREDIENTS BY WEIGHT

(To convert ounces to grams, multiply the number of ounces by 30.)

1 oz	=	¹⁄₁₆ lb	=	30 g
2 oz	=	¼ lb	=	120 g
4 oz	=	½ lb	=	240 g
8 oz	=	¾ lb	=	360 g
16 oz	=	1 lb	=	480 g

USEFUL EQUIVALENTS FOR COOKING/OVEN TEMPERATURES

	Fahrenheit	Celsius	Gas Mark
Freeze Water	32°F	0°C	
Room Temperature	68°F	20°C	
Boil Water	212°F	100°C	
Bake	325°F	160°C	3
	350°F	180°C	4
	375°F	190°C	5
	400°F	200°C	6
	425°F	220°C	7
	450°F	230°C	8
Broil			Grill

USEFUL EQUIVALENTS LENGTH

(To convert inches to centimeters, multiply the number of inches by 2.5.)

1 in	=					2.5 cm		
6 in	=	½ ft	=			15 cm		
12 in	=	1 ft	=			30 cm		
36 in	=	3 ft	=	1 yd	=	90 cm		
40 in	=					100 cm	=	1 m

THE GOOD HOUSEKEEPING
TRIPLE-TEST PROMISE

At *Good Housekeeping*, we want to make sure that every recipe we print works in any oven, with any brand of ingredient, no matter what. That's why, in our test kitchens at the **Good Housekeeping Research Institute**, we go all out: We test each recipe at least three times—and, often, several more times after that.

When a recipe is first developed, one member of our team prepares the dish, and we judge it on these criteria: It must be **delicious**, **family-friendly**, **healthful**, and **easy to make**.

1 The recipe is then tested several more times to fine-tune the flavor and ease of preparation, always by the same team member, using the same equipment.

2 Next, another team member follows the recipe as written, **varying the brands of ingredients** and **kinds of equipment**. Even the types of stoves we use are changed.

3 A third team member repeats the whole process **using yet another set of equipment** and **alternative ingredients**. By the time the recipes appear on these pages, they are guaranteed to work in any kitchen, including yours. **We promise**.